COLLEGE BOUND

COLLEGE BOUND

A Family's Guide to Postsecondary Options for Students with Disabilities

Patricia S. Arter, Tammy B. H. Brown,
and Amy Paciej-Woodruff

ROWMAN & LITTLEFIELD
Lanham • Boulder • New York • London

Rowman & Littlefield
Bloomsbury Publishing Inc, 1385 Broadway, New York, NY 10018, USA
Bloomsbury Publishing Plc, 50 Bedford Square, London, WC1B 3DP, UK
Bloomsbury Publishing Ireland, 29 Earlsfort Terrace, Dublin 2, D02 AY28, Ireland
www.rowman.com

British Library Cataloguing in Publication Information available

Library of Congress Cataloging-in-Publication Data available

ISBN 978-1-5381-9513-0 (cloth : alk. paper)
ISBN 978-1-5381-9514-7 (ebook)

For product safety related questions contact productsafety@bloomsbury.com.

∞™ The paper used in this publication meets the minimum requirements of American National Standard for Information Sciences—Permanence of Paper for Printed Library Materials, ANSI/NISO Z39.48-1992.

CONTENTS

1

WHERE DO WE BEGIN?

At the End!

The process of figuring out what direction to go after high school can be overwhelming. For those with disabilities, it can be an even more challenging task. Recent changes to laws that apply to individuals with disabilities have resulted in more opportunities than ever. However, you may be unaware of the choices available to you. This chapter will help you to know where to begin by helping you identify realistic career goals.

Here are some of the topics you will find in this chapter:

- finding a "just right" job: identifying realistic career goals
- how to set goals
- whom to involve in goal setting
- considering the level of support needed to achieve goals
- taking realistic action steps
- ongoing evaluation of goals

Where do we begin? Yesterday, you were beginning your PK–12 journey, and today, you are ready to graduate. What's next? Where do you want to be next year? Five years from now? What is your overall life goal? What path will get you to that goal? What are your options, and how do you navigate these options to choose what is best for you? There are so many questions to consider! This book is designed to help you think about and answer these questions. It will help to make the journey to achieving your postsecondary goals a smoother one. We will begin by starting at the end. Where do you ultimately want to end up? Let us help you figure it out.

FINDING A "JUST RIGHT" JOB: IDENTIFYING
REALISTIC CAREER GOALS

Chances are that you have heard sayings like "Reach for the stars," "If you can dream it, you can do it," and "Just believe in yourself." Perhaps you have attempted to motivate yourself and give your determination a boost by repeating those encouraging words. But when it comes to finding a "just right" job, determination will only take you part of the way. You also need to have a clear picture of where you are going.

Setting realistic goals is an essential first step in your postsecondary journey. A person with poor spatial abilities (which affect a person's ability to sense direction and estimate distances) would not make a good airline pilot. An individual with weak fine motor skills would not be good at dentistry since they would not be able to move their fingers efficiently in the small space of a person's mouth. And the child who dreams of being a rock star, a YouTuber, or a professional video gamer needs to carefully consider the likelihood of success in such endeavors. Hopefully, you have explored some of these career interests in high school and have a realistic outlook on what you are good at, what you love to do, and what skills you have that can lead to paid employment.

Indeed, with enough grit, it may be possible to succeed in training for a particular job that you are not naturally "wired up" to perform. Maybe you say to yourself, "But I really want to be a dentist," even though you know your manual dexterity skills are not particularly strong. Consider the reality of going to a job day after day and year after year. Consider the reality of that job drawing upon your weakest area. That can quickly lead to discouragement and job burnout. Whether or not you have a disability, exploring a realistic career pathway and getting guidance from those who know you well helps to set you up for long-term career success and independence.

As you begin your journey, develop an awareness of possible careers. Notice the workers you see each day doing various jobs. For example, on a trip to the grocery store, you may see many different employees, including cashiers, stock personnel, deli workers, maintenance workers, customer service workers, and managers. Talk with your parents, teachers, and others about the workers you notice. Think about what the workers' day is like. What tasks do they do? What training did/do they need? What personal qualities make them good at that particular job? Consider things like the level of physical activity, interaction with others, and the working environment. Ask yourself questions like, "What would be the best thing about a job like this?" and "What would be the hardest thing about that job?" You may want to begin keeping a notebook with the jobs you notice and the things you learn about each. Consider, also, what you have already learned; for example, "What job preparation did I gain in high school?" Or perhaps you already have some work experience; "Have I participated in an internship, volunteer work, or paid employment?" All of such preparation and experience can help you narrow your focus.

Taking a good, honest look at yourself is another critical step as you begin your postsecondary exploration journey. There are many online tools to help you assess your strengths and interests, as well as your challenges and limitations. For instance, the O★NET resource center (onetcenter.org/) offers numerous self-assessment tools. You may think you know yourself quite well; however, these assessment tools can often reveal aspects of yourself that you weren't aware of, particularly regarding how these traits relate to future employment options. Such insights can go a long way in helping you identify suitable educational and career goals. Review your individualized education plan (IEP) and transition plan, as well. What are your areas of strength? What are you are interested in and good at? What experiences have made you good at a particular skill? All of these things can help you narrow down your goals.

The Office of Vocational Rehabilitation, or OVR, is another resource that can help people with disabilities who want to go to college or learn a job skill after they finish high school. Most likely, you have made contact with OVR while you were in high school. This is an important step in your journey, because OVR will help you to come up with a workable plan. However, you may not realize that OVR can provide continuing support as you begin to explore educational and job opportunities after high school.

Each state has a department and website with resources for job training available for vocational rehabilitation. Examples include North Carolina's Department of Health and Human Services (https://www.ncd hhs.gov/divisions/vocational-rehabilitation-services); and South Carolina's Vocational Rehabilitation Department (https://www.scvrd.net/). These offices provide evaluations to help determine interests, needs, physical abilities, work history, and aptitude for vocational assessment and career exploration. Vocational rehab centers provide training, resources, and support to individuals with disabilities. Table 1.1 on page 4 shows the ways OVR can help you.

Table 1.1   Office of Vocational Rehabilitation

How can the Office of Vocational Rehabilitation help you?	
What are your support needs?	Based on the postsecondary training you want to pursue, OVR can help you assess your strengths, interests, and support needs.
What will it take to achieve your goals?	OVR can help you create a workable plan. The plan may include finding a suitable school or program, determining the necessary accommodation, and even finding sources of financial support.
Do you need support services?	OVR can provide a variety of support services, such as academic support, job coaching, or assistive technology. Or maybe you need to work through some personal challenges. OVR can help you to find counseling, as well.
Do you need an advocate?	As you pursue postsecondary training, OVR can help clarify your rights, and they can speak up for you if you feel that you have been discriminated against due to your disability.
Are you short on finances?	OVR can help you identify sources of financial support for your training or education. These may include loans and scholarships, but OVR may also be able to help you locate other sources of funding that you were not aware of.
Are you ready to find a job?	Once you complete your education, OVR can help you locate a job that matches your skills and training.

Overall, the Office of Vocational Rehabilitation is there to support you in achieving your goals and becoming as independent and successful as possible in your education and career journey.

Once you feel that you have a pretty good idea of your strengths and challenges, author Yvona Fast (2012) suggests that you honestly ask yourself not only, "Can I overcome this challenge?" but also, "Do I *want* to overcome this challenge?" Choosing not to pursue a particular career path because of the challenges it poses is not a sign of weakness. Such a choice can be a wise decision that promotes future job satisfaction.

As part of the assessment process, think about the level of support the prospective employee would need to succeed once they land a job. Individuals with disabilities have much to offer employers, and some employers like Home Depot, CVS, Walgreens, and Microsoft seek out individuals with disabilities for employment (Solomon, 2020). Such companies offer additional on-the-job support for employees with disabilities. The support may even include a job coach if the individual has an OVR representative.

HOW TO SET GOALS

The best place to begin the goal-setting process is at the end. What do you hope to achieve through your career? Do you aim to live independently and be self-supporting? Or is the primary goal to achieve self-satisfaction by doing something you consider interesting and of value?

Buron and Wolfberg (2008), authors of *Learners on the Autism Spectrum*, suggest a few questions to talk over with your family and others as you aim to set realistic career goals. Whether or not you have autism, the questions can be helpful in figuring out career goals that are a good match for your strengths and interests.

- What do you like to do?
- What interests you?
- What are you good at?
- What do you know how to do?

In addition, envision what you would like your life to look like five years from now and 10 years from now. What would you like to be doing and why is that important to you?

Making goals and knowing in your mind what they are is only a step toward achieving them. You also need to write them down. Why is that important? Because when you write down your goals, you create an important record of the pathway toward success. Also, when you write your goals, you can more easily evaluate them. First, ask yourself, "Are my goals *specific* enough that I would know when I have achieved them?" For example, if the goal is "to get a job as a cosmetologist," would you know when you have achieved that goal? Yes, because there is a clear and specific endpoint. However, the goal of "earning a lot of money" is vague and unclear. Would "earning a lot of money" be $100 or having enough to live on? In addition, evaluate whether or not your goal is *attainable*. Depending on your disability, independent living may or may not be an attainable goal for you. Earning a traditional college degree may be attainable for some but not for others. Begin by stating realistic long-term goals, and then set shorter-term goals that must be accomplished in order to achieve the long-term goals.

WHOM TO INVOLVE IN GOAL SETTING

Some individuals, with or without disabilities, know from the time they are young children what they want to be when they grow up, and they have a reasonable plan for getting there. But most people do not. Whether they are a teen or an adult, most people seeking a new career path can benefit from the guidance of those who love and know them well. Caregivers, family members, and teachers can provide valuable input as you develop long-term career goals. They often have insights about your strengths and challenges, and they may offer a new perspective on a potential career match that you hadn't thought of before, particularly if your heart has been set on a specific "dream job."

It is important to expect that, as family members and others attempt to support you in realistic goal setting, conflict may occur. Michael Bernick and Richard Holden (2015), authors of *The Autism Job Club*, offer a few guidelines for caregivers that can reduce the discord:

- Don't avoid the situation.
- Do avoid telling the individual what to do because the individual may become more determined, or if they follow your advice and it doesn't work out, they may blame you.
- Do ask questions, such as:
  - What would you like to do?
  - How can I help you?
  - I hear you saying _____, but have you thought about _____?
  - Have you considered an alternative such as _____?
- Do offer to help. You might help him or her find more information about a particular job, arrange a talk with someone who knows about a specific field, or provide support as he or she takes steps to develop areas of challenge.

For your part, as the job seeker, be willing to listen to what others have to say. If you disagree with someone's advice, thank them for their input and explain your perspective respectfully. As an adult, you are gaining independence. However, careful consideration of input from those who care about you can help prevent missteps that may have long-term consequences.

CONSIDERING THE LEVEL OF SUPPORT
NEEDED TO ACHIEVE GOALS

Having support can make the difference between achieving and failing to achieve long-term goals. As you begin to write out and evaluate your goals, you should also think about the support that will be needed to achieve them. Identify the people, resources, and accommodations that will be needed at each phase of the process. We will consider available support in more detail in later chapters, but for now, think about these potential resources:

- family members
- friends
- coworkers
- teachers
- university/school personnel
- trainings
- Internet resources
- academic accommodations
- job accommodations

TAKING REALISTIC ACTION STEPS

In addition to setting a goal that is specific and attainable, evaluate whether it is *actionable*. In other words, can you list the steps that would be necessary to achieve the goal? For example, if a person sets a goal of becoming a cosmetologist, steps to achieving that goal would include applying to and getting accepted at a beauty school, passing the required courses, putting in the required number of hours under the supervision of an instructor, and passing the licensure exam.

Action steps needed to prepare for a particular job go beyond academic achievement and job training (Morningstar & Clavenna-Deane, 2018). You may also need to consider areas of personal growth, such as developing social skills or managing anxiety.

ONGOING EVALUATION OF GOALS

Setting a realistic goal is only the beginning! Continue to evaluate the goal as you move forward. Making appropriate changes to your goal as you gain clarity about the demands of a particular pathway is not a failure. It is just part of the process. You may want to keep a notebook or electronic file to track your progress. Keeping a record of your goal-related efforts and discoveries—the contacts you make, impressions about particular postsecondary institutions, and how they fit your needs and goal—can be helpful as you navigate the postsecondary environment.

CONTINUING THE JOURNEY

The journey through your PK–12 years may not have been easy. People with disabilities have been discriminated against for many years. A 1954 Supreme Court decision, *Brown v. Board of Education*, opened doors to make educational opportunities fairer for students who had previously been discriminated against. This court decision laid the foundation for the Individuals with Disabilities Education Act (IDEA), a law that has made public education and appropriate special education services available to students with disabilities. Individuals with disabilities were first guaranteed access to a free, appropriate education in 1975 with Public Law 94-142. Though this law was designed to protect the rights of students with disabilities, access does not always equate with equal opportunity.

TRANSITIONING FROM HIGH SCHOOL

As you enter into a new phase of your education, it's essential to know your rights and advocate for them. The goal of the law (*IDEA*) was to allow you the same opportunities as others (*equity*) with your peers without disabilities (*inclusion*) but also provide extra support in areas where you need assistance (*special education*). Unfortunately, in many schools, special education becomes a "place" rather than a "service." Students with disabilities are often "pulled out" of the general education classroom and sent to another "special class" where they are not able to interact with their nondisabled friends. This may have been your experience for some or all of your PK–12 years. Maybe you were afforded few opportunities to interact with your peers beyond lunch, physical education class, or music class. This is not the intent of the law. However, it is often implemented this way in schools because of convenience, staffing, scheduling, and available resources.

Additionally, you should have been included in your IEP meetings and given a voice to speak, along with your parents, about your strengths, needs, desires, goals, and dreams (*advocacy*). By the time you were 14 years of age, your school should have begun planning for your transition to work or postsecondary education. The individual transition plan (ITP) requires your and your parents' input as to your future life goals, including work, school, and independent living. These goals should have been included in your IEP. This transition plan is meant to guide the courses you take and the job training and experiences you have in high school. The plan should also determine if you will receive a diploma or certificate and if you will go on to some type of postsecondary training. Regardless of if your school included you in this process, these goals will be in your IEP. Your IEP will be a helpful tool to revisit as you plan your future steps. If you don't have one, ask the school for a copy so you have it for your records.

Often, the PK–12 school experience is a bumpy ride, and, unfortunately, things aren't any easier at graduation. Do you want to live independently? If so, how will you pay your bills? What is your employment goal? Do you want to work a paid job? Do your skills and training match the job you are interested in? If not, what type of training do you need? Where do you find help to get the training you need? This process is often daunting, and many fail to get through it successfully. The high unemployment and low independent living rates among individuals with disabilities confirm this.

As an individual with a disability, you are part of the fastest-growing "minority." Recent statistics from the Centers for Disease Control and Prevention (CDC, 2023) show that one in four adults (27%) in the United States have a disability. However, independent living, employment, and postsecondary education outcomes are much worse for people with disabilities than those without. Why? The support you were offered in school often stops at graduation. No one is calling meetings, talking to your teachers, or helping you prepare for work, independent living, or postsecondary training. You and your family are now solely responsible for navigating information and agencies and actively advocating for yourself to find available opportunities and resources.

Prior to 2008, many people with disabilities were expected to take the skills they learned in elementary and high school and seek *supported* (a sheltered workshop: usually for individuals that have cognitive disabilities, piecemeal work under a supervisor with low pay) or *competitive* (seek and interview for a job that has equal pay as a person without disabilities) employment with little or no additional training or support. Though recent changes in the law have increased the opportunities for individuals with disabilities, many individuals with disabilities, as well as their parents and caregivers, are unaware of the available resources and choices. Therefore, the process of navigating educational opportunities after high school may seem overwhelming. We hope this book will help guide you through this process and to become more aware of the resources and choices available to you.

For instance, did you know that you can get support (*accommodations*) for your learning needs at college? If you didn't, you are not alone. While more and more students with disabilities are attending postsecondary institutions, only about 37% report their disability. Even though this support is provided, only 1 in 5 undergraduates reported having a disability in 2015/16; and 15 to 43% of those who do report their disability do not receive accommodations from their school (CDC, 2023). Are students unaware of how to receive these services? Do institutions not provide accommodations? This remains unclear. With the information in this book, however, you can make informed decisions about disclosing your disability, advocating for yourself, and seeking services.

It's important to know what's in your transition plan and your end goal in high school: Will you achieve a diploma or a certificate? Depending on your disability, you may or may not be able to follow a traditional diploma pathway. But even if a traditional diploma pathway is not a good fit for you, you have additional options. In 2008, the Higher Education Opportunity Act opened additional pathways to postsecondary education for individuals with intellectual disabilities that weren't previously available. However, there are few comprehensive transition programs (CTPs), and they are not widely known by the public.

HOW THIS BOOK CAN HELP YOU

This book will help you and your family determine appropriate goals and find the options that are most appropriate for achieving them. Since legislation has changed in recent years, you may be unaware of the available opportunities. Students with disabilities may complete high school and obtain a traditional diploma or a certificate. Inclusive postsecondary education programs (IPSEs) allow you to enter a college training program with a certificate. Many of these IPSEs offer residential, independent living options, and others offer internships with the goal of obtaining competitive employment. Some IPSEs have two-year programs and others have four-year programs. This book will provide guidance to help you understand the laws and safeguards that are in place, as well as the resources needed to navigate the system and choose an appropriate program that best meets your needs.

This is a handbook. That means it is designed to be a resource you can go to again and again, depending on where you are in your postsecondary exploration process and the specific information you need. You may decide to read it from cover to cover, but you don't have to. You may choose chapters or sections to read based on the phase you find yourself in. You may also find that you need to go back to a chapter you read before because you need to understand it better. Throughout the book, you will find checklists, charts, activities, and tips to help you succeed in your postsecondary journey. As you begin this process, you may want to use a notebook to keep track of the checklists and activities, the schools you contact and the people you talk with, questions to ask, your impressions of the schools, and the information you find along the way.

REFERENCES

Bernick, M. S., & Holden, R. (2015). *The autism job club.* Skyhorse Publishing.

Buron, K. D., & Wolfberg, P. J. (2008). *Learners on the autism spectrum: Preparing highly qualified educators.* AAPC Publishing.

Fast, Y. (2012). Career planning for people on the autism spectrum. *Autism Spectrum News.* https://www.autismspectrumnews.org/career-planning-for-people-on-the-spectrum/

Morningstar, M. & Clavenna-Deane, B. (2018). *Your complete guide to transition planning and services.* Paul H. Brookes.

Solomon, C. (2020). Autism and employment: Implications for employers and adults with ASD. *Journal of Autism and Developmental Disorders, 50*(11), 4209–17. https://doi.org/10.1007/s10803-020-04537-w

GETTING STARTED

Directions: *Ask your school for a copy of your individualized education plan (IEP) if you do not have one. Use your IEP to help you record the information. Keep this worksheet in a notebook. Refer to it as you make decisions about what you will do after high school.*

Date of high school completion: _____.

My end goal in high school is/was:
__ A high school diploma
__ A certificate

I completed an internship during high school.
__ Yes
__ No

If you completed an internship:
Where was the internship? _____
What did you do there? *List the tasks here:*

What volunteer experiences have you participated in? (List things like babysitting, helping in church, participating in community groups, etc.)

What subject areas did you do best in when you were in school?

What subject areas were most difficult for you?

What accommodations were put in place to help you succeed in school? (List things like extra time for tests, help organizing larger projects, use of voice recognition software, etc.)

Which accommodations were most helpful to you?

What are your strengths?

What things are difficult for you?

List any medical issues or physical limitations you have:

Do you enjoy meeting new people and making new friends?
__ Yes, I love meeting new people, and I have many friends.
__ Sometimes, but I prefer having one or two close friends.
__ I have difficulty meeting new people and making friends.

What are your hobbies or special interests? What do you most enjoy doing in your free time?

2

WHAT DO THE LAWS SAY?

As an individual with one or more disabilities, you have many rights that are guaranteed by law. However, higher-education laws are not exactly the same as those governing K–12 education. Knowing your rights, as well as your responsibilities, will help you to take full advantage of the many opportunities available to you.

In this chapter, you will find:

- summaries of the laws pertaining to postsecondary education; and
- explanations of what each of the laws means for you and your family.

Recent legislation has resulted in increased opportunities for individuals with disabilities and many choices for postsecondary education. Although you and your family may be familiar with rights in the K–12 environment, the same rules do not always apply in the postsecondary setting. This chapter will help you and your family understand your rights, as well as your responsibilities. It will also help your family know how to support you in your self-advocacy efforts. While related laws will be discussed in this chapter, specific examples of behaviors in the college setting that are covered under the laws will be addressed in chapter 6. Chapter 6 will also address tips for how to manage specific situations.

We begin with a review of the laws. We hope to help you understand your basic rights and help you adjust your expectations for what colleges can and should provide, as well as what they will not provide. We think it is important for you to understand the basics and foundational rules that schools are operating under before we go into more detail throughout the rest of the book. We will also help you know what you can do to help make the transition from K–12 to higher education easier and more efficient along the way.

DISABILITY LAWS APPLICABLE TO HIGHER EDUCATION

The following laws apply to colleges—both public and private. Yes, also private colleges, because most private colleges want to receive federal funding. (Federal funding means that at least some of their students receive student loans and other forms of financial aid from the government.) The laws are designed so that if an organization wants to receive funding from the government, then it must follow the government's laws. Two disability laws will be discussed in the following section. You may already be familiar with them. They are reviewed here to point out some of the differences between the K–12 and college settings. In addition to reviewing disability laws, there are several other laws that we think are important because they apply to colleges and may impact you.

Before disability-related laws were in place, students who needed any sort of specialized help or instruction that differed from what was being offered simply didn't get it. Worse, students with intensive support needs were treated less than humanely and, oftentimes, were institutionalized. As time went on, advocates began calling for change, first on the basic level of treating people more humanely and then at the next level of improved education. That change came in the form of new laws. At the same time, what was known and understood about abilities, learning, and neurodiversity increased, and this knowledge helped to further advocacy efforts and support the changes that have been made over time. The following list is a general overview of the laws reviewed in this chapter.

Every college must have a staff person dedicated to working with students in the area of disabilities. Sometimes colleges have stand-alone offices, and sometimes they are included among other services offered to students. Colleges may use different titles for the employee working in that role. Throughout this chapter, we will call that designated person "the office of disabilities services staff person." Some examples of department titles include Office of Student Support and Success, Disability Services Office, Office of Student Disability Services, Disability Support Services, Disability and Access Services, Accessibility Services, and Services for Students with Disabilities Office.

Table 2.1   Key Legislation

Year and Name of Law	Topic of Law	Explanation
1972 Title IX of the Education Amendments	sex discrimination	School sports programs must not discriminate based on gender and must offer girls as many options as boys.
1973 Rehabilitation Act of 1973, Section 504	disability discrimination	Any organization that receives federal money may not exclude students from their education based on their disability.
1974 The Family Educational Rights and Privacy Act (FERPA)	privacy of school records	School districts and colleges cannot share a student's school records without the student's/family's agreement. In college, this means that the school can only share a student's records with the student's family if the student gives permission.
1975, 1990, 2004 IDEA	disability discrimination in K–12	Only applies to school districts in grades K–12; not college.
1990 Americans with Disabilities Act 1990 Title II (ADA Title II)	disability discrimination	Bans state and local governments from discriminating on the basis of ability.
Fair Housing Act 1968	Emotional support animals in housing	The law separates pets from support animals to allow residents to have an animal in a rented living space even though the owner bans animals.
2011 Title IX now includes sexual misconduct	sex discrimination includes assault and harassment	The 1972 law expands to consider any sort of sexual misconduct a form of sex discrimination.
2021 Behavioral Intervention Guidelines Act of 2021 (not a law yet)	mental health requirements	May possibly become a law but isn't yet. This law will require a college to establish some form of behavioral intervention team, a care team, or a threat assessment team.

Sources for all of the laws in this chapter are located in the resource list.

SECTION 504

The Rehabilitation Act of 1973, Section 504 (referred to as Section 504, or 504) states that "No otherwise qualified handicapped individual shall, solely by means of handicap, be excluded from the participation in, be denied the benefits of, or be subjected to discrimination under any program or activity receiving federal financial assistance." In other words, it is a federal, or national, law that says any organization, like a college, that receives federal funds, like student loans, may not discriminate based on disability. Further, 504 also states that schools "shall take such steps as are necessary to ensure that no handicapped student is denied the benefits of, excluded from participation in, or otherwise subjected to discrimination under the education program or activity operated by the recipient because of the absence of educational auxiliary aids for students with impaired sensory, manual, or speaking skills." In other words, colleges must provide aids, which will be discussed in a later section. Under 504, the existence of an impairment itself is not enough to be considered a disability. The definition requires that it must result in significantly limiting a major daily activity. So, Section 504 protects you from being denied services or being discriminated against because you have a disability. However, you will need to show proof that the disability limits daily activity. We'll explain more about that soon.

What does this mean for you or your family? It means that you should be able to access programs you'd like and qualify for, and that the college staff will work with you to plan to provide you with support.

ADA TITLE II

The Americans with Disabilities Act of 1990 (ADA) contains five different sections referred to as "Titles" that ban state and local governments from discriminating on the basis of ability. In other words, ADA Title II is very similar to 504 but specifically emphasizes that state and local governments cannot discriminate based on disability. ADA Title II addresses, just like 504, the requirement for a college to provide "appropriate auxiliary aids and services where necessary." What this means is that you cannot be discriminated against based on your ability/disability and the college must provide you with reasonable services you need to be successful. Additionally, the US Department of Education's (DOE) Office of Civil Rights (OCR) also states that "students with disabilities who are auditing classes or who otherwise are not working for a degree must be provided auxiliary aids and services to the same extent as students who are in a degree-granting program" (DOE–OCR, 2021). This means that students working toward a certificate program but not a degree still must be provided with accommodations.

There are two exceptions to the ADA Title II law. The exceptions, meaning the right of nondiscrimination, are if the student is currently using illegal drugs or if the student is evaluated to be a direct threat to others. It is not uncommon for college students to experiment with illegal drugs. If a student is caught doing so by college staff or the police, he or she can lose the right of nondiscrimination. "Current illegal use of drugs means illegal use of drugs that occurred recently enough to justify a reasonable belief that a person's drug use is current, or that continuing use is a real and ongoing problem."

College is a place where students are learning to manage their own emotions. There may be extreme situations when a student is not able to manage his or her emotions to the point that the student may threaten or harm someone or be a "direct threat." "Direct threat" is defined as follows: "Direct threat means a significant risk to the health or safety of others that cannot be eliminated by a modification of policies, practices or procedures, or by the provision of auxiliary aids or services." In this case, regardless of whether the student has a documented disability or not, he or she will be evaluated to determine if he or she is a threat to others. If that happens and the student has a disability, then the rights to nondiscrimination are lost. A possible consequence in both cases—drug use and threatening behavior—is separation from the college (suspension or dismissal). In most colleges, dismissal is forever, but suspension is for a defined length of time. This means it may be possible for the student to return to school with the rights to nondiscrimination back in place.

What does this mean for you or your family? This means the same as what 504 means: you should be able to access the programs you'd like and qualify for, and college staff will work with you to plan to provide you with support. It also means that you must follow the law regarding drug use. In addition, it means that you cannot behave in a manner that is threatening to others.

YOUR CHOICE TO INFORM OR NOT

It is every student's right to decide whether or not to inform the college of a disability. In 2022, only about 33% of students with a disability decided to disclose their disability to their college, according to the National Center for Education Statistics (NCES), which is part of the US Department of Education's Institute of Education Sciences (IES) (NCES, 2022). Of course, the only way to receive any sort of accommodations or assistance with a disability is to inform the college and follow their instructions. The instructions will include turning in paperwork and meeting with staff to talk about what you need and want. However, it is your right to not use any supports that are available.

What does this mean for you or your family? This means that you have a decision to make, and we encourage you to work with your family to decide what is best for you and your goals. There are many reasons why someone would not want to use aids, such as a desire for an increased sense of independence or confidence. The reason we wrote this book is to help you learn about all that is available for your use, so that you can make informed decisions. It is important to note that many nondisabled college students utilize their school's resources in one way or another—utilizing the tutoring or writing centers, attending counseling sessions, using student health services, or working with a fitness trainer or academic mentor. Students who are more engaged on campus and utilize the supports are generally more successful at reaching their goals.

ACCOMMODATIONS

Accommodations, or auxiliary aids, are tools that can help you access and/ or understand material. Aids can be things like devices that help you read or see the computer screen better, a keyboard that is easier to manipulate, large-print materials, or amplifiers. Unlike your high school experience, you the student, not your family or teachers, have to request auxiliary aids (accommodations). And you must ask for help in a reasonable timeframe. This allows enough time for school processes and staff planning to put the request in place. For example, if you need an FM (frequency modulation) system, you cannot request one the day before classes begin because the staff needs time to get the equipment, make sure it works correctly, and plan for getting the device to you or your classroom. The staff person(s) or department name that you make such a request to differs from college to college. There is, however, often a specific office on campus that manages academic accommodations—and *disability support* or *access* are the usual words within the department names. If the request is for something other than academics or your classes, the person or department to request it from may differ depending on what you seek help for. For example, you may need to speak with the housing office if you need help with accessing your room and the physical plant office for help find your way around campus to avoid stairs, or you may need to talk with the dean of students if you are unsure with whom you should speak.

After a request for accommodations (help or support) is made, the college may ask you for supporting documentation, such as results from diagnostic tests or professional evaluations. How and where the documentation comes from will vary by school. In some cases, colleges may have their own services to conduct the evaluations; in other cases, you may have to use a specific company; or it may be your responsibility to decide who provides the testing. Your IEP from high school can be part of the documentation that is provided to the school, however, the old IEP itself will not be enough to document the disability. The IEP information can sometimes provide useful information about what accommodations have been most effective for you in the past. Check the date of your most recent IEP or test/diagnostic results from the end of high school. The requirements of colleges vary, but it is possible that test results from the last year of high school will be accepted. Sometimes you can use old IEP or test/diagnostic results, which means little to no cost to you.

Once the request for accommodation is completed and then reviewed by the college, you will be notified of the accommodations that will be provided. Some examples for your classes may include a quiet space to take tests, extra time to take tests, or extended deadlines on assignments. Auxiliary accommodations can also include things like another student acting as a note-taker in class, an interpreter, or equipment to assist with tasks like screen reading.

ANIMALS ON CAMPUS

Colleges must allow you to bring your service animal with you anywhere you go on campus, a right guaranteed under the ADA law. Service animals are trained to perform a service for the owner. If you will live on campus, we encourage you to make the housing office aware so that, in the event that one more or your peers are severely allergic to animals, rooms can be assigned to meet everyone's needs. The housing or physical plant office can also help determine where the animal can relieve itself. You do not, however, need to seek approval to bring the service animal. Your service animal cannot be denied.

Support animals, on the other hand, do not meet the ADA definition of a *service* animal. A support animal's purpose is to help with the owner's mental health struggles, such as anxiety, depression, or post-traumatic stress disorder (PTSD). Unlike service animals on campus, there are specific steps a student must go through to get approval to bring their support animal to campus, starting with the disability services and the housing office. Providing documentation from a professional counselor or psychiatrist may be part of the approval process. Support animals will have limits as to where they can and cannot go with you. Typically, they are restricted to the student's living quarters and may not attend class with the student. There may be other guidelines to follow such as using assigned laundry machines that those who have severe allergies know to avoid.

What does this mean for you or your family? Now is the time to think about what things have been most helpful to you in your schoolwork. Make a list of things that you think you would like to continue using in college. Also, include on the list any other things that you think would be helpful but that you haven't been able to try. After you are accepted to the college, make an appointment with the office of disabilities services staff person. There you can find out the specific steps your college wants you to take and what paperwork you must give them. With this staff person, you will talk about what kinds of aids and support can be provided. Bring your list of ideas with you to help with the conversation. (See worksheet at the end of this chapter.)

You must be able to care for the service or support animal when you bring it to campus. Your college will not provide helpers to care for the animal. Be aware of disturbances your animal may cause for your peers and try to minimize them; typical complaints college staff may receive about animals on campus include odor, noise, allergies, and aggressive behavior.

FAIR HOUSING ACT

The Fair Housing Act is a law that prevents discrimination against people trying to buy or rent a place to live. One of the pieces in the law allows support or service animals, even if all other animals are banned from that living space. This law applies to your campus's residence halls, viewing students as renters. The law allows your college to require you to submit a letter from a doctor or counselor before being allowed to have the support animal in your residence hall room. The Fair Housing Act falls under the US Department of Housing and Urban Development, and any complaints can be filed at 800-669-9777.

MORE NONDISCRIMINATION LAWS

ADA Title III addresses public accommodations and includes classrooms, residence halls, sports complexes, and theaters to ensure students' access to these buildings and rooms. ADA Title V states that a student with a disability can choose not to accept any accommodations; in other words, students are not required to use the accommodations.

What does this mean to you and your family? We already discussed your right not to tell the college about your disability. However, Title V law means that when you do decide to tell them and a plan is made, you still have the choice of which supports or aids to use. You are not required to do everything the college suggests. There are always consequences to every action, of course. If you decide not to use a support but then do poorly on a test, you cannot go back to ask to do it again with the aid that you declined. You can always change your mind and start using an aid partway through the semester, but you cannot go back and change what has already been completed in your schoolwork. In all cases, the decision is yours to make.

WHAT THE LAWS DO NOT COVER

Colleges and universities are not required to provide you with a personal assistant to help with personal care like bathing, dressing, eating, and so on. The law states: "Personal aids and services, including help in bathing, dressing, or other personal care, are not required to be provided by postsecondary institutions." Going to college can mean living with family while being a college student or it can mean going away and living somewhere other than your family's home. It is possible to go away to college and have a personal attendant. However, the college will not pay for or help you find an attendant.

The 504 regulations also state: "Recipients [meaning the college] need not provide attendants, individually prescribed devices, readers for personal use or study, or other devices or services of a personal nature. Title II of the ADA similarly states that personal services are not required" (US Department of Education, Office of Civil Rights, 2021). This means that colleges are not required to provide you with special equipment for your personal use, outside of class or in addition to basic living conditions. For example, the college does not have to provide you with a device to use for entertainment in your room on the weekend to help you watch your favorite show.

Colleges are not required to make changes that "fundamentally alter the nature of a service, program, or activity," meaning that accommodations and supports can be offered to assist a student with access and completing a task, but the college will not change the content of a course or assignment. Many college courses are hard, designed to help students learn subjects and content that is challenging to understand, synthesize, and use. The difficulty level of a course will not be altered as an accommodation. Some college classes will require certain physical activities. A drawing, sculpture, architecture, or nursing class requires students to work with specific materials. Aids or supports may be possible in some cases, but the class will not change the requirement for students to be able to successfully build a model or give a patient an injection as part of their grade.

In providing supports or accommodations, colleges are able to say no to a specific request if that request will "result in an undue financial or administrative burden" (DOE–OCR, 2020). In other words, the aid or support cannot cost so much money that the institution cannot afford it. The definition of a burden in the law is very broad, so it is open to what different people think it means. What might be too expensive for one college to handle may be very different at another college. Assistive technology to help read a computer screen is certainly a reasonable aid. Asking the college to buy you a wheelchair is a request that most likely will not be approved. Asking for a room or a private bathroom to be newly constructed and added to an existing residence hall will not be approved. Requesting an existing room with a private bathroom for certain disabilities may be approved. You may follow the typical process to request to live on a specific themed floor (such as a gaming-themed residence floor or an international-culture residence-themed floor), and that floor must be accessible, wherever it is located. However, a request to move the themed floor to a different building that is more convenient will not be granted.

What does this mean for you or your family? If you want to go away to college and live on campus, there are many things to talk about with your family. Students are actually only in their classes for 15 to 18 hours a week. That leaves students a lot of time outside of class. Talk with your family about what kinds of things you think you will need. Knowing what the college may and may not provide can help you understand what to seek from other sources and help you decide what types of colleges and programs to which to apply.

More laws are reviewed in the following section to help you in your college experience. Knowing your rights and responsibilities through being aware of the following laws can assist you in understanding the college culture.

FERPA

The Family Educational Rights and Privacy Act (FERPA) is a privacy law that applies to PK–12 education. FERPA also applies to colleges. FERPA covers who is permitted to know about your official school records. School records are things like grades, health records, and student behavior conduct files. Unlike in high school, you are now the only owner of your records, and you choose who can see them, including your guardians or families. Now, your family needs your permission to be informed of your progress, even if they are paying for you to attend. Families working with specific campus offices and employees may only be informed of your records if you have given specific permission, typically by signing a form provided by the college. Even with your permission, know that the college is not *required* by FERPA to work with anyone other than you. Knowing all of this, it is still very common for college students to sign the form so that their families can hear about their records.

What does this mean for you or your family? Patience and planning! Meeting with school staff ahead of time to talk about a working relationship is a proactive step to take. Most school employees in student services or student affairs departments are very willing to work with families. They are also dedicated to you being involved in order to learn self-advocacy. College employees are oftentimes frustrated by families who exclude the student in discussions of their own experiences or rob the student of practice at solving their own problems. Learning these skills is part of a college education.

Sometimes families who are advocating for their students make it clear that they think the classroom experiences are all that make up the students' education. However, all of the out-of-class time greatly contributes to what and how students learn. For instance, working with a campus department to get a question answered or to work out a problem helps students develop communication and problem-solving skills and may help to increase students' self-confidence. Both of these skills should be developed as part of your education. Skills that are needed for any sort of self-advocacy in many different situations, even the boring and inconvenient ones, all contribute to your college education and development toward independence.

There are many exceptions to the privacy given by FERPA. Schools may publish directory information, but students can decide to keep their information unpublished. Directory information contains things like your name, email address, and phone number. Another exception to keep in mind is that staff must follow the instructions of any sort of legal request for your records, like police or any court order, if they are asked for access. Staff may also disclose personal student record information in a health or safety emergency. The definition of a safety emergency refers to big events, such as a pandemic or a shooter on campus. The definition of a health emergency is in the case of being taken to the hospital for some reason. In other words, staff can notify families if you are hurt (health/safety) or caught violating liquor laws (legal). Last, college employees may share your records with other employees, but only if they need to know specific details in order to do their jobs.

GUARDIANSHIP OR CONSERVATORSHIP

You become independent (your own self-guardian) automatically when you reach the age of 18 or enroll at a college no matter your age. Most students have the type of relationship with their families that involves assistance with decision-making as they make the slow transition to becoming an adult, all without any legal or formal processes through the courts. Sometimes families are surprised that the college considers their student a legal adult even if the family is paying tuition and the student still very much depends on his or her family. The legal term *guardianship*, or *conservatorship*, is used to describe the person who is legally appointed to be a decision-maker for you. That person can be a family member or a professional guardian. *Guardianship* or *conservatorship* can only happen if you and your family apply for it. The difference between the two terms depends on the state you live in, but they are very close in meaning. Pursuing guardianship or conservatorship can be an expensive and emotional process through the court system, as it will be the court, not you, that decides if you need a guardian or not and why.

Some benefits of guardianship or conservatorship include:

- protection in looking out for your best interest;
- assistance with decision-making;

- help connecting to resources; and
- continuity of care between big transitions in life, like from high school to college and college to work.

Some negative things about guardianship or conservatorship include:

- loss of autonomy or independence;
- the possibility that you don't agree with the guardian's decisions, but are unable to change them;
- legal fees involved in guardianship or conservatorship; and
- the possible feeling of being stigmatized by the legal statement that you are incapacitated and in need of a guardian.

What does this mean for you and your family? If you and your family are considering guardianship or conservatorship, we encourage you to very carefully consider the decision and what you will try to accomplish with it before taking action. We also encourage you to learn about other options that offer support in decision-making while still allowing you to keep some independence. Resources may vary by state. For example, Pennsylvania can have an appointment of a representative payee who is a legally recognized helper in managing any of your public benefits such as Social Security Disability (SSD) and Supplemental Security Income (SSI). Another Pennsylvania-appointed role is a health care representative—who can be a family member or a trusted friend of yours—who will lead you in making any health care and medical decisions (Disability Rights Pennsylvania, 2018). Power of attorney is also a way to give decision-making power over parts of your life, like finances or health care. This book provides you with resource information about where to begin, but in all legal issues, you should consult with a lawyer prior to making a decision or a plan.

HIPAA

Student records, including treatment records from a college clinic's doctor, psychologist or psychiatrist, are considered under FERPA but not under HIPAA. HIPAA is the Health Insurance Portability and Accountability Act of 1996. Even though they may provide health clinic services to students, colleges and universities are not considered "covered entities" under HIPAA. As long as the person is a student, then FERPA privacy laws are what apply.

What does this mean for you and your family? Sometimes college staff may be confused about what law applies to your records. If you ever find yourself in a situation where the college will not release your records because of HIPAA, you can request that they research which law applies to your situation as a college student using this source provided by the US Department of Health and Human Services: https://www.hhs.gov/hipaa/for-professionals/faq/518/does-ferpa-or-hipaa-apply-to-records-on-students-at-health-clinics/index.html.

TITLE IX

Title IX is a federal law that addresses any sort of sex discrimination that may prevent a student from pursuing an education in the PK–12 setting. The same law also applies to the college setting. It applies to both employees and students and states, "No person in the United States shall, on the basis of sex, be excluded from participation in, be denied the benefits of, or be subjected to discrimination under any education program or activity receiving Federal financial assistance." Originally put into place in 1972 to address the discrimination faced by female athletes, the law has since expanded to include all forms of sexual misconduct, from harassment to rape. Institutions are expected to inform the school community of these expectations, grievance processes, contact people, and support resources.

What does that mean for you or your family? You should know that you have the right to pursue your education free from any form of sex discrimination, including harassment. It is also important to know that you have the responsibility to behave toward your peers in a manner that is appropriate. Understanding social cues to guide behavior in the case of liking a potential romantic partner is important in this context. Being able to communicate preferences is a needed skill. Another needed skill is the opposite: being able and willing to comply with someone else's stated boundaries. Expectations of specific social behaviors will be discussed in chapter 6.

Similar to a required ADA staff person, each institution is required to designate a Title IX coordinator, and most have also designated deputy coordinators. Most institutions have detailed complaint (grievance) processes in place to manage violations that can be found in the student handbook or the college's website. The complaint process can be formal or informal, and it is up to the person filing the complaint to decide which path to take. Anyone can file a complaint with the institution, which must investigate it. The Title IX coordinator or deputy coordinators are the people to contact to seek specific campus information and referrals to other resource people if you ever need support. The Office of Civil Rights (OCR) within the US Department of Education (DOE) is the agency that manages Title IX. Complaints about an institution not following the law can be addressed to OCR@ed.gov or 800-421-3481, TDD (telecommunication device for the deaf) 800-877-8339.

BIG: BEHAVIORAL INTERVENTION GUIDELINES (FUTURE LAW)

At the time of the printing of this book, the BIG (behavioral intervention guidelines) law has been presented to both chambers of Congress and is in committee. While most colleges and universities already have some form of behavioral intervention team, care team, or threat assessment team, this new law will help to formalize what these groups do and further support strengthening training and practices. These teams of college staff are people who listen to and address concerns about specific students expressed by others in the college community. An example of a concern is a faculty member who has noticed that one of their typically cheerful students has been very withdrawn, sad, and angry and has also changed the way they dress in the last two weeks. The team will see if anyone else has concerns about this same student and look for patterns. They may then reach out to the student to see what sort of help is needed. The goal is to help students who may not be seeking it for themselves.

WHEN THINGS GO WRONG

Institutions must address any sort of harassment, discrimination, or rule-breaking that takes place that is directed toward a person because of his or her disability. There will be grievance or complaint processes in place to address concerns. The college or university employee who is the office of disabilities services representative or the dean of students' office will be good resources on where to seek information about how to begin the complaint process. In order to move forward in the complaint process, the harassment or discrimination must be serious enough that it can stop the student from participating in his or her education. Of course, the college must be aware or be made aware of what is happening. If the college is aware but does nothing to improve the situation, then you may file a complaint against the college. The Office of Civil Rights, which is located within the Department of Education, is the US government entity that enforces 504, ADA laws, FERPA, and Title IX. A complaint may be filed with OCR by

emailing: OCR@ed.gov; or
faxing: (202-453-6012); or
mailing:

US Department of Education
Office for Civil Rights
Lyndon Baines Johnson Department of Education Bldg.
400 Maryland Avenue, SW
Washington, DC, 20202-1100

Contact 800-421-3481 to confirm receipt of your correspondence

What does this mean for you and your family? If you feel that you are being discriminated against while in college, then you can file a complaint. There are two kinds of complaints. If you feel that a person is treating you with bias, then you can file a complaint with the college's complaint process. The college itself wants to hold its employees and students to high standards and to nondiscrimination, and they are able to hold individual people accountable through their processes. If you feel that the college itself is discriminating against you, then you file a complaint with the OCR.

INFORMED STAFF

In addition to needing to comply with laws, institution staff have resources to support them in their work to be able to continuously improve services to students. All colleges (that receive federal funding) with 15 or more employees must designate a Section 504 coordinator, though the person's job title may differ. You can expect college staff in the disabilities service office to have a general understanding of students with disabilities and understand the laws and available resources. In many cases, they are excited to work with students with disabilities. While they are school employees, they are in their role because they have a passion for helping you succeed. It is reasonable to expect that they should also be experienced in working with instructors on how to provide helpful situations for students in their classes. The office of disabilities staff person is most likely connected to a network of professionals who support each other in providing accurate and up-to-date support to students. In fact, colleges may offer much more support to students than the minimum stated in the laws. There are many national, state, and regional organizations that help support and provide continuing education to the campus staff people working with students with disabilities and also provide support to students and their families. Many support networks and professional associations were specifically founded for the purpose of strengthening the education experience of students with disabilities. A few of the national organizations are listed below, but there are certainly more that are not covered in this list. In addition, your state and region may have additional supports to check into.

SUPPORT NETWORKS AND PROFESSIONAL ASSOCIATIONS

- Association on Higher Education and Disability (AHEAD) acts as a clearinghouse to help people connect with resources (https://www.ahead.org/about-ahead).
- Accessing Higher Ground is an AHEAD annual conference focused on courses and online learning accessibility (https://accessinghigherground.org).
- DREAM (Disability Rights, Education Activism, and Mentoring) is part of AHEAD and is a national organization with individual clubs on college campuses for college students with disabilities (https://www.dreamcollegedisability.org).
- HBCU Disability Consortium was a coalition made of up staff from historically Black colleges and universities (HBUC) focused on striving for excellence in serving students with disabilities (https://hbcudisabilityconsortium.org). The group's work has now changed into Black Disabled and Proud: an online resource for college students which also is part of AHEAD (https://www.blackdisabledandproud.org).
- National Center on College Students with Disabilities (NCCSD) a federally funded national organization, this group serves college students with disabilities and those who work with them (https://nccsd.ici.umn.edu/).

- ATHEN is made up of college staff and faculty dedicated to improving accessibility for everyone in higher education (https://athenpro.org/).
- Coalition on or Disability Access in Health Science and Medical Education advances leading practices to increase access for people with disabilities in health science (https://www.coalitiondahse.org/#:~:text=Coalition%20for%20Disability%20Access%20in%20Health%20Science%20Education%20(Coalition%20DAHSE)&text=The%20Coalition%20was%20founded%20on,disabilities%20in%20Health%20Science%20Education).
- Think College National Coordinating Center is a group that works to improve college experiences for students with disabilities and does so by collecting data and resources. They keep a list of college programs for students with intellectual disabilities (https://thinkcollege.net/about/what-is-think-college/think-college-national-coordinating-center9).
- COPAA Council of Parent Attorneys and Advocates is a nonprofit organization that focuses on the rights and education of students with disabilities (https://www.copaa.org/page/about).

DEFINITIONS

Ableism is a term for being biased against people with disabilities. Bias can range from underlying individual beliefs that show up as microaggressions to outright discrimination. Ableist actions and beliefs can come from an individual level or from a system-wide level. Someone can have ableist views and beliefs without having discriminated against anyone. The term discrimination refers to actions that block someone from their rights, in this case the right to education.

Allyship is a term for people who do not have a disability but do support and advocate for equity and inclusion of people with disabilities. Allies use their privilege, meaning the fact that others are willing to listen to them, to challenge the way things currently are and push for improvements.

Neurodiversity is a term that refers to a range of natural variations of how the human brain works. Instead of viewing people who are outside of typical neurodevelopmental patterns as having a deficit, it emphasizes the value of these differences and promotes acceptance, understanding, and accommodation. Examples are people with autism, ADHD (attention deficit hyperactivity disorder), dyslexia, and Tourette's syndrome. Neurodiversity is a framework that promotes that diverse ways of thinking and experiencing the world can add to the richness of the human experience and should be celebrated and not cured.

SUMMARY

Understanding what to expect from colleges will help you and your family make decisions about your future. You do not have to memorize these laws. Do try to remember that these resources are here for you to refer back to any time you need them as you move forward along your college journey.

RESOURCES

Congress.Gov. (2022). H.R.2877—Behavioral Intervention Guidelines Act of 2021
117th Congress (2021–2022). https://www.congress.gov/bill/117th-congress/house-bill/2877/text
Disability Rights Pennsylvania. (2018). *Chapter 10: guardianship in Pennsylvania.* https://www.disabilityrightspa.org/wp-content/uploads/2018/04/CCSDM-11E.pdf
National Center for Education Statistics. (2022, April 26). *A majority of college students with disabilities do not inform school, new NCES data show.* https://nces.ed.gov/whatsnew/press_releases/4_26_2022.asp
US Department of Education, Office of Civil Rights. (2021). Auxiliary aids and services for postsecondary students with disabilities. https://www2.ed.gov/about/offices/list/ocr/docs/auxaids.html
US Department of Education, Office of Civil Rights (2020). Disability discrimination. https://www2.ed.gov/policy/rights/guid/ocr/disability.html
US Department of Education, Office for Civil Rights. (2021). Family Educational Rights and Privacy Act (FERPA). https://www2.ed.gov/policy/gen/guid/fpco/ferpa/index.html
US Department of Education, Office of Civil Rights. (2020). Students with disabilities preparing for postsecondary education: Know your rights and responsibilities. https://www2.ed.gov/about/offices/list/ocr/transition.html
US Department of Education, Office for Civil Rights. (2021). Title IX and sex discrimination. https://www2.ed.gov/about/offices/list/ocr/docs/tix_dis.html and https://www2.ed.gov/about/offices/list/ocr/transition.html

US Department of Health and Human Services. (2022). Summary of the HIPAA Security Rule. https://www.hhs.gov/hipaa/for-professionals/security/laws-reg ulations/index.html

US Department of Justice Civil Rights Division. (2016). Americans with Disabilities Act Title II Regulations. https://www.ada.gov/law-and-regs/regulations/title -ii-2010-regulations/#:~:text=Title%20II%2C%20which%20this%20rule,State %20and%20local%20government%20entities

KNOW YOUR RIGHTS

Directions: *Select the law that governs each scenario. You may use the listed laws more than once.*

Scenario

1. __ Each day, a fellow student in your science class comments on your "sexy shirt" and follows you to your dorm room, making comments about your body. You've told the student to stop, but the behavior continues.
2. __ You meet the admission requirements for a federally funded college, but your application is rejected because you use a wheelchair.
3. __ Your parents call the school and ask to speak to your math professor about your recent test grades.
4. __ A professor tells you that you can't bring your service dog to class.

Law

a. The 1974 Family Educational Rights and Privacy Act (FERPA)
b. Title IX
c. Section 504 of the Rehabilitation Act of 1973

Checklist

__ Check the dates on your current documents for your IEP or diagnostic tests.
  • What was the start date? _____.
  • When do they expire? _____.
__ Make sure you have a copy of all documents, including IEP and diagnostic tests.
__ Make a list of things that you would like to continue using in college to support your learning. Include any other things that you think would be helpful but that you haven't been able to try.
__ Decide if you will live in campus housing or not.
__ Decide if you will disclose your disability or not.
__ Decide if you will pursue any sort of guardianship or conservatorship or any legal support people.

__ Plan to visit campus; set meetings with the following offices:
- Admissions
- The office of disabilities services staff person
- Be sure to talk to other students while there
- Housing office

__ Plan to attend the new student orientation
- FERPA forms can be signed at new student orientation to allow the college staff to share your education records with your family.

3

WHAT KINDS OF PROGRAMS ARE AVAILABLE AND HOW DO I CHOOSE?

Many individuals with disabilities and their families don't think college is a possibility. That simply isn't true! Today, more than ever, postsecondary education is accessible—cognitively, socially, physically, and financially—to everyone. There are many new laws that make college admission possible for individuals with disabilities. This chapter will discuss the types of postsecondary programs available, help you find the right fit for your goals, and provide resources to help you navigate the process.

Before you read this chapter, you may want to take a look at this resource. It is a great way to get started! https://thinkcollege.net/family -resources.

Topics covered in this chapter include:

- what to consider when choosing a school;
- four-year colleges;
- two-year colleges and vocational schools;
- comprehensive transition and postsecondary (CTP) programs or inclusive postsecondary education (IPSE) programs; and
- financial aid.

FOUR-YEAR COLLEGES

The first type of college we will review is the one with which you may be most familiar: the four-year college and university. If you have not considered applying to a four-year college, know that about 20% of all

37

undergraduate college students report having a disability (National Center for Education Statistics [NCES], 2023). A four-year college offers a bachelor's degree, which can take as little as four years to earn if you attend full-time (12 credits per semester or more), though sometimes it takes longer. There are several different types of four-year colleges that we will describe here.

ONLINE VERSUS IN PERSON

Some colleges are online with no in-person experiences. Others are mostly in person but offer online programs or individual online courses. When deciding which colleges and programs to apply to, online or in person is an extremely big difference for you to consider. Think about if you are a self-starter, organized, and an independent worker. If so, online programs may be best for you. They are convenient and efficient but do not allow for much social experience.

Are you interested in meeting new people? Do you like to learn by hands-on and face-to-face experiences? Do you want to experience "college life"? If so, then perhaps in-person classes are best for you. Be sure to check how classes are offered before you register.

FOR-PROFIT OR NONPROFIT? PUBLIC OR PRIVATE?

Some colleges are not-for-profit, and some are for-profit, like a regular company. For-profit colleges are a little bit harder to learn about, because many of them keep their formulas for success a secret, much like a company hides its trade secrets to get ahead of the competition. The approach that these two different types of colleges take toward support and service to the students can vary greatly. Also, some for-profit colleges may seem less expensive than nonprofit colleges because of the way they present themselves to prospective students, but sometimes they are actually more expensive in the long run. The majority of colleges are not-for-profit. When deciding which colleges and programs to apply to, for-profit or not-for-profit status is a very big difference for you to consider.

Not-for-profit colleges can be either public or private. Public colleges receive the majority of their funding through the state government. Most states have one large state college, and many also have a state system of several colleges. State colleges are considered an extension of the state and always have to follow that state's laws. Private colleges receive most of their funding from student tuition and donations. Private colleges, of course, also have to follow the laws, but they have more freedom than state colleges in some of their operations. When deciding on which colleges and programs to apply to, a private or a public college may feel different when you visit, but it is not typically a big difference on which to base your decision.

Among the private colleges, there are more categories that are determined by the culture of the college or its mission and purpose. Also, the nature of the college's founding group can also impact the type of college it is. For example, there are religious and nonreligious colleges. The category of *religious college* does not mean that all attending students are studying to work in some type of religious job. Rather, it means that the founders of the college were affiliated with a specific religious group, such as Catholic, Protestant, or Jewish, and may have specific values to which the college, including employees and students, aspire. When you visit, you can get a sense of how individual colleges have their own feel and culture. Depending on your own beliefs and those of your family, when deciding which colleges and programs to apply to, the choice between a nonreligious or religious-based college may be very important or it may not be the main category on which to base your decision.

SIZE

Another category in which colleges differ is size—not only the size of the campus(es) but also the student population, programs, and facilities. Some colleges can have fewer than 1,000 students. The biggest colleges can have more than 70,000 students on one campus. Depending on the school, some campuses have more resources than others. The biggest difference for students in college size tends to be in personal preference. Some students want to join a community of a specific size. Some like to be at a smaller college, where there is a higher likelihood of one-on-one attention from faculty and staff, and they can be around the same people every day. Others like to be at a larger place where they can be a bit more anonymous and blend in with the crowd or take part in large-scale events. Most small colleges do not have huge classes, while larger colleges may have classes with 200 or more people in one lecture hall. Students in large lecture classes may rarely, if ever, interact personally with the professor, though sometimes teaching assistants are available to meet with students who need extra support.

Larger colleges tend to have more options in courses, resources, and activities. Sometimes students pick a college based on what they *do not* want. For example, the thought of a very large school may be overwhelming to one person, and the thought of a small school may feel suffocating to the other. Getting around campus, of course, is greatly impacted by the college's size. Larger colleges often have shuttle buses to assist students' travel between classes, residence halls, parking lots, and other parts of campus. However, not all colleges offer that type of convenience. When deciding on which colleges and programs to apply to, size is typically a big factor on which to base your decision.

LOCATION

A college's location is another category to consider. By location, we mean if the college is in a city, a town, or a cornfield. Some colleges blend into the middle of a city, and some are completely isolated from the nearest town. A college's location will determine many different aspects of the campus experience, such as what services are easily available off campus. The college's location will also impact transportation—transportation around campus, transportation around town, and also transportation from campus to home. By location, we also mean what part of the country the college is in. Many students wish to stay within a specific radius of the place they call home. For example, a student may want to be no more than three hours away from his or her family. Another factor to consider is the *geographic* location of the college; this will impact the weather and/ or landscape you will have to navigate. Students can see the beach from some colleges. Some colleges have underground tunnels so people can move around campus without going out into the cold and snow. Some colleges are in areas that have flat lands or steep hills. The list goes on. And preferences vary greatly. So, when deciding on which colleges and programs to apply to, location is typically a big factor on which to base your decision.

Also, know that location impacts tuition costs. In-state tuition is usually less expensive than out-of-state tuition. Additionally, if you go to college out-of-state, you will need to consider room and board and the expenses of not living with your family.

COMPETENCY-BASED PROGRAMS OR LIBERAL ARTS?

Some colleges specialize in competency-based programs that focus on individual timelines that students progress through as they master specific skills. Most colleges, however, require a predetermined list of courses to complete specific programs or majors. Students pick their major according to the career they wish to pursue. Many times, students choose colleges to apply to that offer the specific major they need for the career they wish to pursue. There are a wide range of majors, and every college offers a different mix. If students do not know what major they want when applying to the college, they can base the decision on the other criteria listed in this chapter. In this case, many colleges categorize such students as "undeclared" or "undecided," with the understanding that they will confirm their major after completing a certain number of semesters (or credit hours).

Each major or program has specific entrance requirements that applicants need to meet in order to enter the program, continue in that program, and graduate from that program. Some program requirements include a minimum grade point average (GPA) and participation in internships. Some majors will require students to go to specific places (like education majors going to local schools or nutrition majors going into hospitals) and interact with specific people (to start working with future clients). Some majors require specific physical activities that are related to the target job, such as nursing majors administering injections, occupational therapists moving patients, and architecture and art students manipulating materials. When deciding which colleges and programs to apply to, the majors they offer and the requirements those majors ask of you are big differences to consider.

LIBERAL ARTS OR PROFESSIONAL PROGRAM?

Another category to consider is the liberal arts–focused college or the professional program-focused college. A liberal-arts-focused college aims to help students become well-rounded citizens. Some of the courses that may be required in a liberal arts college may seem unrelated, specifically, to your major, such as philosophy, sociology, or a foreign language. However, such courses can be valuable in helping students open their minds and think more broadly in order to contribute to society. Technical or professional colleges focus on preparing students for their career or a specific job. Many colleges have a mix of liberal arts and specific career preparation. When deciding which colleges and programs to apply to, a college's specific focus is typically tied to students' decisions about their major and career path. Many students do not really consider this category consciously when making their decisions.

One difference to note between a liberal arts college and a professional program is that you can earn a degree from the four-year (liberal arts) college. Then, depending on the career path you want, you may have to pass professional licensure or certification tests. Ideally, the college program prepares you, the student, to pass such tests; however, licensure tests are not given by the college. On the contrary, they are administered through the specific profession toward which you want to work. Usually, a college's pass rate for the licensure exam of a particular program is posted on the college website. If you have a look at these statistics, the percentage of students who pass the licensure exam can be an indicator of how well the college's program prepares students for that particular career.

RESEARCH OR TEACHING FOCUSED?

Other categories of colleges include research-level schools—meaning, the school's faculty either focus on teaching students or conducting their own research. Research-focused colleges typically have teaching assistants instructing the courses, while the faculty spend much of their time on research projects. Non-research-focused schools, also called teaching-focused colleges, typically have faculty who try to continuously improve their teaching skills.

COLLEGE ATHLETICS

Many students base their college decisions on being able to play a specific sport. College athletics are broken down into three divisions. Division I (Division One) is typically what you see on TV. A student is recruited to a college, first, to play his or her sport, and second, to be a student. If the student is a very talented athlete, he or she can receive scholarships to cover college tuition. Such a student is typically not involved in other campus activities and can sometimes get paid for his or her athletic talents. On the opposite end, Division III (Division Three) sports make up half of all college athletics. Division III colleges do not give scholarships to athletes. Students are considered *student-athletes*, and their coaches prioritize students' academic performance. Division II colleges are the in-between or a mix of Division I and Division III.

There are also a lot of club sports and intramural sports on campuses, meaning that students can play on a recreational team in their free time and have fun with their friends. When deciding on which colleges and programs to apply to, athletics can make a very big difference for some students, and, for others, it won't make any difference in the decision-making.

OTHER CONSIDERATIONS

There are a few other things to consider when deciding on a four-year college. Many colleges offer five-year or combined three/two-year programs where students are guided through a specific list of courses to earn a bachelor's degree and then also a master's degree in a shortened period of a five-year span. Otherwise, it will typically take a year or two longer to earn both degrees. Another option to shorten the time in college is to take AP, or advanced placement, courses in high school that can count toward college requirements. There are also some high schools that have relationships with local colleges where students can take a college class during their regular high school day.

Four-year colleges offer several advantages for individuals with disabilities.

- **Support services**: Four-year colleges have specific offices dedicated to disability support services. These offices help to document your need for various accommodations and communicate these needs to course instructors. The office can provide resources such as note-taking assistance and accessible technology. The office can also help you make special arrangements, such as getting extended time on tests.
- **Flexible scheduling**: These colleges often offer flexible scheduling options, including evening, weekend, and online classes. This flexibility can be helpful if you need to schedule around doctor's appointments or if you rely on others for transportation.
- **First-year support**: The transition from high school to college is a big one! Many four-year colleges have programs and services specifically designed to help students as they learn to navigate the world of higher education. Some colleges offer special programs for first-year students. Others offer courses, such as "University 101," where students learn about the college community and develop skills that

will help them to succeed in the college environment. Some colleges have staff or full departments dedicated to the first-year transition or the new student orientation program.

- **Diverse programs**: Four-year schools typically offer a wider range of programs than other types of schools.
- **Social engagement opportunities**: Four-year colleges usually host a wide variety of clubs and activities that provide many opportunities to connect with other students who have similar areas of interest. Most four-year colleges have staff who are dedicated to planning events that help students get to know one another and have a sense of belonging in the college community.
- **Career preparation and guidance**: Some students begin college without a clear idea of what they want to major in. Four-year colleges provide career services that include career counseling and a variety of interest assessments that can help you determine a major that matches your interests and abilities. In addition, a four-year college degree may allow you to access a career that you would otherwise not be qualified for. A person with a bachelor's degree can earn a lot more income over a lifetime than a person without. But even having a degree doesn't guarantee a job! Your colleges career services office, or the equivalent, can help provide networking opportunities and sometimes even assistance with job placement.

WHAT DO TWO-YEAR COLLEGES AND VOCATIONAL-TECHNICAL PROGRAMS OFFER?

A two-year college is sometimes known as a community college or junior college. The programs offered by a two-year college can typically be completed in two years or less, though it can take longer for students who attend part time. Some of the programs lead to an associate's degree. Two-year colleges provide a variety of majors. Many courses taken at a two-year college can be transferred to a program at a four-year college. (However, it's wise to make sure this is the case if transferring to a four-year school is your goal.)

Two-year colleges also usually provide some specialized programs, some of which can be completed in less than two years. Such programs may lead to a diploma, certificate, or preparation for licensure requirements, rather than a degree. These programs usually have a vocational or technical focus that prepares students for specific careers in fields such as health care, automotive, or culinary arts.

The two-year or community college offers many advantages. Since the courses are usually less expensive than a four-year college, the two-year college can help to reduce the overall cost of your education. But, if your goal is to transfer to a four-year school, be sure to see if the two-year school has a transfer agreement with the four-year school you want to transfer to. Otherwise, some of your courses may not count toward your degree. If you are unsure about your career path, a two-year school can be a good place to take courses to gain a better idea of your interests. The courses will also give you a good idea of how prepared you are for college-level work. Another advantage of the two-year colleges is that they usually offer various support services, such as writing and tutoring centers.

Tip: If there is no transfer agreement with the four-year school you want to attend, your academic advisor can give you guidance on courses that *usually* transfer. However, keep in mind that the advisor cannot guarantee acceptance of the courses.

Tip: Writing and tutoring centers are not just for students who struggle. Be sure to take advantage of academic support services! Students are often paired with tutors who have taken courses with the professor of the relevant subject. Though you can always request an appointment with your professor when you have questions, student tutors are generally more accessible, and they can help clarify the professor's expectations for assignments.

A two-year college is usually closely tied to the community in which it is situated. Its mission is to offer a variety of programs that meet the educational needs of students within the community, as well as the career needs of the community.

Many two-year colleges have transfer agreements with four-year institutions. If you want to begin at a two-year college, but your goal is, ultimately, to earn a bachelor's degree from a four-year institution, find out which schools, if any, they partner with. This will save you time and money in the long run because when schools have transfer agreements, one school agrees to accept comparable courses for transfer credit. Without this agreement, you may find out too late that your new school does not accept your previous coursework.

Two-year colleges and vocational-technical schools offer several advantages for individuals with disabilities:

Table 3.1   Programs Typically Offered by Two-Year Colleges

Associate's Degrees	Associate's degrees are usually completed in two years and require the completion of about 60 credit hours of coursework (or approximately 20 courses). The program consists of some general education courses and some courses in the major field.
Transfer Programs	Some two-year colleges have transfer agreements with four-year colleges. Students complete the first two years of a four-year program at the two-year school and then transfer to the four-year school to complete the bachelor's degree in a particular field of study.
Career and Technical Education (CTE) Programs	Many two-year colleges offer vocational and technical programs that prepare students for jobs in fields like health care, automotive technology, culinary arts, or welding. Though some programs lead to an associate's degree, some lead to diplomas or certificates. Some also prepare students to take a licensure exam in a particular area.
Adult Education	Many two-year colleges provide classes that prepare adult learners for their high school equivalency (GED) exams.
Continuing Education	Classes to help professionals stay current with certifications like CPR are also commonly offered at two-year schools.
English as a Second Language	Classes for non-native English speakers who want to improve their English language proficiency will usually find courses for beginners and more advanced English learners.
Remedial Classes	Students who feel underprepared for college-level work can take remedial courses in basic skill areas like writing, reading, and math.
Noncredit Classes	Two-year colleges often provide personal enrichment courses on areas of interest, such as photography, fitness, or cooking. The courses do not count for college credit but are provided as a service to members of the community.

- **Accessibility**: Two-year colleges tend to be situated in the student's local community. Some students with disabilities find it more comfortable to attend school in a location that is familiar and where they have the support of friends and family. In addition, attending classes in your home community can make it easier if you have frequent doctor or therapy appointments.
- **Small class sizes**: Compared to larger universities, two-year colleges typically have smaller class sizes. The lower student-to-teacher ratio can make it easier to interact with your instructor and get personal attention.
- **Support services**: Many two-year colleges have as part of their mission supporting students who are underprepared for the rigors of college-level work. As a result, two-year colleges usually have a

strong network of support for students who wish to take advantage of it. Individual or group tutoring centers provide academic help for all coursework. Writing centers often provide group instruction, peer-review, and/or one-on-one support for those who struggle with writing and those who just want to make sure their paper is the best it can be.

- **Cost-effective education**: Community colleges are often more affordable than four-year institutions, making higher education more accessible to individuals with disabilities who may face financial challenges. Additionally, some students with disabilities may be eligible for financial aid or scholarships specifically for students with disabilities.

- **Career and vocational training**: Two-year colleges often offer vocational and technical programs that provide hands-on training for specific careers, such as certified nursing assistant (CNA), commercial driver (commercial driver's license [CDL]), auto technician, and heating-ventilation and air conditioning (HVAC) technician. These programs can be especially valuable for individuals with disabilities who may benefit from specialized skills training and job placement support.

Overall, two-year colleges can provide a supportive and inclusive environment for individuals with disabilities, offering affordable and convenient opportunities for education, skill development, and career preparation.

WHAT IS A COMPREHENSIVE TRANSITION AND POSTSECONDARY (CTP) PROGRAM OR AN INCLUSIVE POSTSECONDARY EDUCATION (IPSE) PROGRAM?

A comprehensive transition and postsecondary (CTP) program and inclusive postsecondary education (IPSE) both provide students with intellectual and developmental disabilities (I/DD) opportunities to access higher education but differ in their structure and focus. Some of the most popular are THINK programs. These programs are housed within a college campus community.

A great resource for your college search is https://thinkcollege.net /college-search. The site lists CTP/IPSEs by state and explains what is offered. These programs generally have an application and interview process. Some offer residential, as well as commuter, options.

It's important to note that these programs are very specifically designed for individuals with intellectual and developmental disabilities who have a history of special education services during K–12. In fact, a person must have an I/DD to be admitted to a CTP or IPSE. This is not the case with the four-year and two-year programs that are open to all individuals with disabilities who meet the admission criteria. To qualify for a CTP or IPSE, an individual must have I/DD and be unable to get a traditional college degree in a two- or four-year program. Individuals with I/DD can be admitted to a CTP or IPSE if they have a certificate of attendance or an alternative diploma.

Often the terms CTP and IPSE are used interchangeably but there are some differences. Comprehensive transition and postsecondary (CTPs) programs are specialized postsecondary programs designed to support individuals with I/DD in pursuing higher education and transitioning to independent adulthood. These CTPs provide structured curriculum and individualized support to help students develop academic, vocational, and independent living skills for college and beyond. Key features include a structured curriculum, individualized support, transition services, inclusive environments, and collaboration with community partners.

Comprehensive transition and postsecondary (CTPs) programs:

- are specifically designed to provide students with I/DD a comprehensive college experience;
- often offer specialized coursework, life skills training, and career development specific to the student's needs;
- typically have a structured curriculum with a focus on skill-building, independent living, and employment readiness; and.
- offer a mix of traditional college courses and modified courses to meet the needs of students with disabilities.

Inclusive postsecondary education (IPSE) provides opportunities for individuals with I/DD to participate in postsecondary education alongside their nondisabled peers. These programs focus on inclusion, independence, and employment skill development. They also offer a range of supports to ensure success for students with disabilities in college settings. Supports may include academic accommodations, peer mentoring, specialized instruction, and access to campus resources and services. The goal is to create inclusive environments where students with I/DD can successfully pursue their academic and career goals alongside their peers.

Inclusive postsecondary education (IPSE) programs:

- focus on integrating students with I/DD into existing college courses and campus life alongside nondisabled peers;
- emphasize inclusion and participation in all aspects of college life including social integration and academic enrichment; and
- enable students to audit or enroll in regular college courses with additional support from program staff or peer mentors.

These programs provide opportunities for I/DD individuals to attend college and universities with their nondisabled peers and participate in employment skills training, internship experiences, independent living, and social events. Some IPSEs provide residential opportunities as well. Most programs are two to four years and culminate in a certificate.

In summary, while both CTPs and IPSEs promote higher education opportunities for students with I/DD, CTP programs offer specialized curriculum and support services while IPSEs focus on inclusive integration into existing college environments with appropriate support.

THE IMPORTANCE OF POSTSECONDARY EMPLOYMENT TRAINING

Getting a good job helps people live better. To find a job, you need training and help finding work and workplaces that treat everyone fairly. But for people with disabilities, it's often harder to get a job. According to the Bureau of Labor Statistics (2024), the employment rate for people with disabilities was significantly lower than those without disabilities, with only 21.3% of people with disabilities employed compared to 65.4% of people without disabilities; additionally, the unemployment rate for people with disabilities was 7.6%, considerably higher than the 3.5% rate for people without disabilities. Why? Well, some people with disabilities don't get the right education and training. Others face unfair treatment because of their disability. Some employers think people with disabilities can't work as well as others or require special accommodations that the company isn't willing or able to provide. Indeed, even if they get a job, people with disabilities might need individualized help, like coaching or special equipment. Unfortunately, sometimes this help isn't easy to find. Finally, some people with disabilities worry that if they work, they'll lose benefits or health care. This makes them less likely to get a job.

WHAT DO CTP/IPSES DO TO PROMOTE
JOB SKILLS AND EMPLOYABILITY?

Both Ctps and Ipses are important for helping people with intellectual disabilities learn job skills and find work. These programs have lessons and training that focus on things like talking at work, being polite, managing time, and solving problems. They also teach skills needed for different types of jobs that someone might like. Some programs let students try out jobs or watch other people work so they can learn. This helps them feel more confident about working.

In these programs, students get help with finding job openings, preparing for interviews, and doing well at work. They might have someone called a job coach to help students learn on the job and keep doing well. They also help students figure out what kind of job they might like and how to find an opportunity in that area. Sometimes, these programs work with local businesses to help students get jobs and hold events during which students can learn about job opportunities and network. Overall, these programs help students learn skills and get support so they can find and keep a job and become more independent at work.

IPSE and CTPs offer several advantages to students with I/DD:

- **Accessibility**: In addition to having accessible facilities, including ramps, elevators, and accommodations for individuals with mobility impairments, IPSE/CTPs have disability support services offices on the college campus that provide resources such as note-taking assistance, alternative testing arrangements, and accessible technology. Most IPSEs have a staff person who provides overall program support including creating a person-centered plan with academic, independent living, social, and employment goals. The program provides individualized support by meeting with students and families, assisting instructors in making academic accommodations, providing specialized classes in social skills and independent living, conducting employment training, and advocating for student access services on campus. Most also provide additional peer mentor support in and out of class for academic, social, independent living, and employment skills.
- **Flexible scheduling**: These programs often offer flexible scheduling options based on students' individual needs. Often, there are

specialized classes, and most academic classes are audited. This flexibility can be beneficial for individuals with disabilities who may have challenges with traditional schedules due to medical appointments, therapies, or other needs.

- **Individualized support**: IPSE/CTPs often offer specialized instruction in social skills, functional academics, nutrition, independent living, and employment training. Peer mentors assist in residential life, like making meals or eating at area restaurants, and integration into the campus community like going to social events, academic tutoring, and job coaching. This can provide a more supportive learning environment, allowing for personalized attention and accommodations based on individual needs yet gaining and maintaining independence.

- **Transition support**: Many IPSE/CTPs recruit from area high schools and provide tours and application assistance in the last year of high school. Be sure to check with your special educator or school counselor and/or begin your search here https://thinkcollege.net/college-search.

- **Cost-effective education**: IPSE/CTPs are often more affordable than postsecondary options as the program determines its fees. If it is an approved IPSE, students and families are eligible for federal funding like FAFSA and Pell Grants. Additionally, there are often state grants for individuals with disabilities to cover the costs of the program. This makes higher education more accessible to individuals with disabilities who may face financial challenges. Additionally, some students with disabilities may be eligible for financial aid or scholarships specifically for students with disabilities.

- **Career and vocational training**: IPSE/CTPs focus on employability skills as a key component of their curriculum. Often job shadowing, interning, job coaching, interview skill practicing, and résumé building are part of the specialized classes. Many IPSEs/CTPs have agreements with vocational and technical programs that provide hands-on training for specific careers, such as childcare assistant; welder; certified nursing assistant (CNA); auto technician; and heating, ventilation, and air conditioning (H-VAC) technician. These programs can be especially valuable for individuals with disabilities who may benefit from specialized skills training and job placement support.

FINANCIAL AID

College expenses: There are very few instances where college is free for all attending students. Colleges have several different things for which they charge. Students are typically billed for each session or semester. The bill includes a price for tuition, which is the main expense, and sometimes referred to as *block tuition*. Block tuition allows students to take between four and six courses each time, instead of charging per course. If the student lives on campus, there will also be separate charges for room and board: room, meaning housing, and board, meaning a meal plan. Students living on campus are normally required to pay for a meal plan. Colleges also charge a wide range of additional charges such as a general fee, an orientation fee, a health insurance fee, a student activities fee, and a graduation fee that all students are required to pay to attend. Fees can also be attached to specific majors, depending on the supplies or extra expenses the program necessitates. Such fees can range from a few hundred to a few thousand dollars. The cost of buying or renting your books is not listed on your college bill, but they are still expenses you will need to manage. Other expenses of going to college that are not listed on your college bill can include personal things such as your phone, internet, entertainment (going to movies or restaurants), and other popular luxuries such as getting your nails done.

TYPICAL EXPENSES

- tuition (covers between 4 and 6 courses—a full-time semester)
- room (if living in campus housing)
- board (if using, or being required to use, a meal plan)
- general fees
- books and supplies
- personal expenses

Financial aid: Because college is extremely expensive, most students receive some type of financial aid to pay for it. Financial aid is a broad term used to cover a number of different types of funding to help pay college tuition. For each college you apply to, individual students are awarded a financial aid package that is often comprised of different types of funding. The financial aid package can be based on need, which is determined according to your family's income, and it can be based on merit, which is determined by your past performance in different areas. Each college will use your application and the completed FAFSA to determine your financial aid package. Your financial aid package will be different for each college you apply to. Therefore, for each college you apply to, you will have a different set of expenses as well as a different financial aid package. Many students decide on which college to attend according to how much they have to pay after the financial aid package is applied to the college bill. Some students will not even consider applying to any private colleges assuming that their tuition prices are not affordable. However, what the majority of students and families do not realize is that many private colleges automatically offer discounts, scholarships, or grants to students that can make them comparable in cost or even less expensive than many public colleges. Gather your information before assuming that your choices are limited.

FAFSA: Any student wishing to receive financial aid for college expenses must complete a form called the FAFSA, or Free Application for Federal Student Aid. The website to apply for FAFSA is https://studentaid .gov/h/apply-for-aid/fafsa. If you are planning to go to college, you should complete the form, even if you don't think you will qualify for financial aid.

The government form is notoriously complicated and will require information from your family's tax forms. Be sure to begin the form several months to a year in advance of when you need the aid. The FAFSA is completed each year by a specific deadline to apply for the following year's expenses. It will be the college or state that sets the deadline. FAFSA deadlines by state can be found here: https://studentaid.gov/apply-for-aid/fafsa /fafsa-deadlines. Once you decide on your school, look into its financial aid office, which may offer assistance to students and families with applying for aid. Helpful information and frequently asked questions can be found here https://www.collegemagazine.com/a-dummies-guide-to-fafsa-and-finan cial-aid-in-college/.

TYPES OF AID

Merit-based versus need-based: Need-based aid is about finances. Need is typically judged according to the income of whomever you are a legal dependent of. Typically, that is your family. If your parents are divorced, the aid will depend on how your parents' taxes are filed. The FAFSA is used to determine need. Merit-based aid is about your performance or record. This may include high school grades or scores on tests such as the SAT or ACT.

Other things that can also be considered are the service work the student has done and, perhaps, talent in a certain area (such as art or music).

DEFINITIONS

Grants: Aid that students do not pay back. Grants are typically based on financial need.

Scholarships: Aid that students do not pay back. Scholarships can be based on financial need or on merit or talent. Scholarships can come from within your own college, and you may not even have to apply for them. Other scholarships are awarded from outside organizations and include an application process.

Loans: Aid that students must pay back. There are many different kinds of loans. Some of them are backed by the government and will appear on your college bill as part of your financial aid package. Others will be up to you and your family to obtain to cover what your financial aid does not. All loans have an interest rate (the amount a lender charges a borrower for the loan, over time). Borrowers must begin to pay back some loans as soon as the month after obtaining them, but students commonly do not begin to make payments on most college loans until approximately six months after leaving college. All loans are different, and you must take special care to be sure you know the specific conditions under which you borrow the money.

Work-study jobs: This means the student works a part-time job on campus to cover some of their expenses. First, the student qualifies for the work-study job through their financial aid package. Students who qualify for a work-study job are not automatically assigned a job. The student must find, apply, and interview for the job on their own. What categorizes a campus job as "work-study" is where the paycheck comes from. The funding of the pay comes from the government and is considered part of a student's financial aid package. The paycheck then goes directly to the student and is not automatically applied to the student's college bill. There are also some part-time jobs on campus that the college pays for. Students can hold these jobs too, but they are not listed on any financial aid packages.

Table 3.2   Scholarship Opportunities and Resources for Paying for College for Individuals With Disabilities

Description	Link
Paying for college: Think College	https://thinkcollege.net/resources/resources-by-topic/paying-for-college
Medicare waivers	https://thinkcollege.net/think-college-news/medicaid-support-for-higher-education
Disability scholarships	https://www.scholarships.com/financial-aid/college-scholarships/scholarships-by-type/disability-scholarships
Intellectual disabilities scholarships	https://thinkcollege.net/resource/scholarships/scholarships-for-students-with-intellectual-disabilities
	With downloadable PDF Ruby's Rainbow for individuals with Downs Syndrome—$5,000 to $10,000 https://rubysrainbow.org/
	Autism Can Do—$1,000 to $5,000 https://johnscrazysocks.com/pages/autism-can-do-scholarship-2024
	Wells Fargo Scholarship Program for People with Disabilities https://learnmore.scholarsapply.org/pwdscholarship/

RESOURCES

Bureau of Labor and Statistics. (2024, February 22). *Persons with a disability: Labor force characteristics—2023 press release.* https://www.bls.gov/news.release/pdf/disabl.pdf

National Center for Education Statistics (NCES). (2023, TBA). Table 311.10. Number and percentage distribution of students enrolled in postsecondary institutions, by level, disability status, and selected student characteristics: Academic year 2019–20 [Data table]. In *Digest of Education Statistics.* US Department of Education, Institute of Education Sciences. Retrieved December 5, 2023, from https://nces.ed.gov/programs/digest/d22/tables/dt22_311.10.asp

CHOOSING A COLLEGE: WHAT'S IMPORTANT TO ME?

Directions: For each of the following criteria, decide whether it is very important to you, somewhat important to you, or not important to you. Place a checkmark in the appropriate box.

Table 3.3   What's Important?

College Criteria to Consider	Level of Importance to Me		
	Very Important	Somewhat Important	Not Important
Living on campus			
Living at home			
Distance between home and campus			
Availability of public transportation			
Campus location (e.g., in my state)			
Liberal arts–based or competency-based program			
Faith-based program			
Financial aid			
Cost of the program			
Length of the program			
Online classes			
In-person classes			
Flexible scheduling			
Support services			
Internship opportunities			
Opportunities for social interaction			
Opportunity to get a college degree			
Hands-on training for a job			
Sports			
Size of the college			
Class size			
Opportunities for tutoring and extra help with coursework			

4

HOW DOES THE ADMISSIONS PROCESS WORK?

The admissions process can be challenging for all students, but for those with disabilities, it can be a formidable task. For some programs, the process and requirements are the same for students with and without disabilities. In such cases, the student needs to determine whether or not to disclose his or her disability and, if choosing to disclose, when to do so. Other types of programs have admission requirements that are specific to the program's field of study.

Topics in this chapter include:

- the admissions process;
- gathering the appropriate information for admission to a college; and
- for families, how to support your student through the application process.

AN OVERVIEW OF THE ADMISSIONS PROCESS

Once you have decided on a particular type of college, it is time to begin the admissions process. The admissions process varies slightly depending on the type of program you choose, but these are the usual steps in the process:

1. **Check admission requirements**: Each college or university sets its own admission requirements. Most require a high school diploma or its equivalent (such as a GED), transcripts (an official

copy of your grades from high school or any postsecondary schools you have attended), letters of recommendation, an essay or personal statement, and a completed application form. Some colleges also require standardized tests, like the SAT or ACT exam. Some specialized programs like music and art require portfolios or recordings of your work.

2. **Take standardized tests (if required)**: Some colleges require applicants to take either the SAT or ACT exams, but not all schools do. Exam requirements are more common to four-year colleges than other types of schools. Check to see if the school you wish to attend requires a specific exam. If so, the school may also require applicants to achieve above a minimum score.

3. **Complete the application**: Fill out the application form for each college you're applying to. Applications are usually available on the school's website. Complete the application carefully and be sure to proofread it before you submit. It's a good idea to have a family member or friend review your application just to be sure you don't have any spelling or grammar errors. The application process usually requires additional materials in addition to the application form. Sometimes the application will not be reviewed by the school until all materials are submitted, so be sure to read all of the instructions carefully. It's a good idea to make a list and check off each item as you attend to it.

4. **Submit transcripts and test scores**: Arrange for your high school transcripts and, if required, official test scores (SAT/ACT) to be sent directly to the colleges you're applying to. If you took any classes at a postsecondary school, the college will probably expect official transcripts of that, as well. When requesting transcripts, you may notice the terms "official transcript request" and "unofficial transcript request." "Official" transcripts are those sent directly from one institution to the other, without passing through the hands of the student. "Unofficial" transcripts are sent directly to the student or are accessed online by the student. Because of the potential for students to attempt to alter their grades, most colleges require "official transcripts." Some schools charge a fee for transcripts to be sent.

5. **Gather and submit additional application materials**: Collect and submit all necessary application materials. Keep in mind that gathering these materials takes time. Request letters of

recommendation from people who know you well and can speak to your ability to succeed in the program you are applying to. Be sure to give people enough time to respond. Many colleges have online forms for the recommender to complete rather than requiring a letter. Those who do require a letter may want the person to submit it directly to the college rather than giving it to the student. Give the recommender information about how to submit the recommendation, as well as any deadlines. (Remember to thank people who take the time to write a recommendation for you!)

6. **Write an essay or personal statement**: Many colleges require applicants to write an essay or personal statement as part of the application process. This is your chance to showcase your personality, explain unique experiences you have had, and discuss your goals. Tailor the essay/statement to each college you are applying to, considering specific prompts, questions, requirements, or any other elements that each institution expects from its applicants. Proofread your work carefully!

7. **Apply for financial aid**: Whether or not you believe you qualify for financial aid, it is a good idea to complete the Free Application for Federal Student Aid (FAFSA). This application allows you to apply for funding through the federal government. Many schools use this information to make decisions about the aid or scholarships they will provide.

8. **Receive the admission decision**: After submitting your applications, you'll receive admission decisions from the colleges you applied to. Check the school's website to find out how they communicate their decision. Many notify students through the postal service or email. In addition to the admission decision, the admissions office may notify you of missing materials or important deadlines, so be sure to check mail and email frequently if you are not in the habit of doing so. Review acceptance letters carefully for any additional steps required to secure your spot. You may need to submit a deposit or respond in some way to confirm your plan to attend.

9. **Acceptance and enrollment**: If you are accepted to more than one college, compare financial aid offers and other variables, such as those covered in table 3.3, and decide on which college to attend. Follow the enrollment instructions provided by the college

to confirm your acceptance. You will likely need to pay an enrollment fee to confirm your decision to attend. Be sure to attend to
deadlines.

10. **Attend orientation and register for classes**: Once you have
decided which school to attend, plan to take advantage of orientation sessions offered by the school. These are important sessions
that are designed to help new students get off to a good start by
familiarizing them with campus resources and student life. Orientation can also be great opportunity to meet the faculty and academic
advisors for your program. Most likely, if you are attending a four-
year or two-year college, someone from your program will help
you to complete a schedule and register for your first semester of
classes. During orientation, schools often provide opportunities for
social interaction with other incoming students so that you can
connect with future classmates and begin to make new friends! The
school may also include helpful sessions for your family members
to attend.

MORE ABOUT ORIENTATION

New student orientation programs are designed to help all students who are
new to college to prepare to begin the experience. Programs vary between
schools. Some college orientation programs only focus on academics, such
as explaining your schedule and other paperwork related to your studies.
Other colleges manage the same academic pieces but add informational
and social and family programs as well. In all cases, we strongly encourage
you to participate in whatever type of orientation program your institution
offers.

Academic-related activities in an orientation program may involve
placement exams for courses, such as math and foreign language. Typically,
students receive their first-semester schedule of classes. You may be able to
make changes to your schedule, if desired. Most colleges will have already
prepared your class schedule by the time you arrive, so you don't get to
create it. Many schools also include your academic advisor in the experience in some way.

Other tasks that are usually addressed during orientation include
the completion of paperwork, such as signing financial aid forms and an
opportunity to sign the waiver form. If you have a car, you will probably

be able to get a parking pass. (This will save time, as lines can be long at the beginning of the semester!) You will also have the opportunity to have your photo taken for your student ID. Again, doing so during orientation will likely be much quicker than waiting until school begins.

Colleges that are very large or that are highly selective (meaning they're very hard to get into) typically hold their orientation programs a few days before the semester begins. Some may include a summer session that may be virtual. Smaller or less selective colleges often hold their orientation programs either a few days before school starts or in the summer. Some colleges will do programming for students to help them adjust to college. Programs may explain campus resources or opportunities to get involved, such as honors programs, clubs, service work, work-study jobs, and study abroad opportunities.

It's important to note that the admissions process can vary based on factors such as the college's admission policies, the competitiveness of the applicant pool, and the specific requirements of the program or major you're applying to. Always refer to each college's official admissions website and contact their admissions office if you have any questions or need clarification on the application process.

Sometimes admission to a college or university does not necessarily guarantee admission to a particular program. Certain programs, such as those in the field of education or health care, may have additional admission requirements. For example, in some schools, students may have to wait until the end of their sophomore year to apply to a particular program like teacher preparation or nursing. This sometimes has to do with state licensure requirements that the college must follow. The college may have to verify that a student has successfully maintained a minimum grade point average (GPA) after taking a specified number of credits, passing basic skills testing, or completing courses in the specific subject matter before they can be admitted to the program.

APPLYING TO TWO-YEAR COLLEGES AND VOCATIONAL TRADE SCHOOLS

The application process for two-year or community colleges and vocational trade schools is generally similar to that of a four-year college. However, four-year colleges and universities may be more competitive and have stricter entrance requirements than two-year or vocational trade schools.

Two-year colleges and vocational trade schools often have as part of their mission providing access to postsecondary education for those who may be underprepared for the rigors of a traditional four-year college program. So, for example, whereas a four-year institution may have minimum score requirements on standardized entrance exams, the two-year college may provide several options: achievement of a minimum standardized exam score, a passing score on a placement test administered by the two-year college, or the successful completion of a remedial course (usually in math, reading, or writing) before taking additional courses in the program of study.

WHEN TO APPLY

Deadlines matter! Be aware of application deadlines for each college. Submit your applications and all required materials well before the deadlines to ensure they are processed on time.

Some schools have *rolling admissions*. This means that the school or program allows students to begin to take classes at the start of any semester. However, some schools or programs must be begun at the start of the academic year, which is usually the fall semester.

Online coursework is sometimes accelerated with courses being six to eight weeks in length. Therefore, students in online programs sometimes have more flexibility in when to begin their program, as such courses begin more frequently. However, remember that such courses are usually presented in an accelerated format, meaning the same workload as a traditional semester-long course has to be completed in a brief period of time, so fewer courses are taken at one time.

APPLYING TO COMPREHENSIVE TRANSITION AND POSTSECONDARY (CTP) PROGRAMS OR INCLUSIVE POSTSECONDARY EDUCATION (IPSE) PROGRAMS

An inclusive postsecondary education (IPSE) program provides opportunities for individuals with intellectual and developmental disabilities (I/DD) to go to college like everyone else. They learn work skills, do internships, and hang out with friends. Some programs even have places to live on campus. These programs usually last from two to four years and give out certificates for completion. These programs offer special certificates that can help students get jobs.

Some programs are called comprehensive transition and postsecondary (CTP) programs. They started after a law called the Higher Education Opportunity Act (HEOA) was passed. This law allows students to get federal financial aid to go to school. CTPs are only for students with I/DD and are approved by the US Department of Education. Any student wishing to receive financial aid for college expenses must complete a form called the FAFSA, or the Free Application for Federal Student Aid. The website to apply for FAFSA is https://studentaid.gov/h/apply-for-aid/fafsa. Chapter 3 discusses this more completely.

The admission process for CTP/IPSE programs are similar and follow some of the same steps as two- or four-year colleges, but there are usually special admission requirements. The Think College website https://thinkcollege.net/college-search lets you search for IPSE programs by state. It will tell you if the program is two or four years, if it offers residential options, and if it is a CTP that is approved for financial aid.

It's a good idea to go to an open house event or tour the IPSE program and meet with the staff prior to applying to ensure it's the right fit for you. It's important to go to the program's website, where the admission guidelines will be listed. For example: https://www.winthrop.edu/ceshs/winthroplife/. On this website, you will learn a bit about the program and find links to contact someone for information, set up a tour, or apply.

Remember that most CTP/IPSEs are programs on larger college campuses. Students attending these programs are required to follow all the same university policies and procedures as other students. Students have access to the same campus services and offices as traditional students, with additional resources from the CTP/IPSE program, including a main point of contact, usually a coordinator or director, peer mentors, and academic/social/residential support.

SPECIAL IPSE/CTP ELIGIBILITY AND ADMISSION CRITERIA

- student must be 18 to 25 years of age
- record of special education services throughout K–12
- record of intellectual or developmental disability
- previously enrolled in high school program that does not lead to traditional diploma or does not allow for traditional college admission

- demonstrates adequate communication skills and socially acceptable behavior
- ability to navigate independently
- personal goals of independent living and/or employment
- motivation to learn

ADMISSIONS PROCESS FOR IPSE/CTPS

1. **Review the program's website and schedule a meeting or tour**: Program staff can help you determine if you meet the admission requirements before you apply. One example of a CTP website is: https://www.winthrop.edu/ceshs/winthroplife/.
2. **Complete application**: The application may be online or in paper form. It usually requires personal information and may require recommendations from your teachers and proof of disability. Some will also include surveys for you and your family to fill out to help determine your goals and if the program is right for you. (See the appendixes to this chapter for more information about applying for an IPSE)
3. **Interview**: Most programs will require video and/or an in-person interview where the staff will ask you questions about what you are interested in, your goals, and things you can or cannot do on your own. You can have your parent or family at the interview, but the questions will be asked of you. Parents and family members are encouraged to come to support you, but they cannot answer questions unless the applicant requests their input. (See appendix for types of questions they may ask in an interview.)
4. **Course selection**: Once you are accepted, staff will meet with you and your family to do person-centered planning. You will decide on the classes you will take and create your schedule. You will also need to decide if you will be a residential or commuter student. (See appendix: ICE cube and Alex ICE.)
5. **Orientation**: Most programs will have a program orientation before the college orientation. Some may bring you to campus a day or two before the other students arrive.

Remember that you are a student of the college first and then the program. You should attend all new student orientation events to learn about the college campus and services.

WHAT DO INDIVIDUALS WITH DISABILITIES NEED TO CONSIDER WHEN APPLYING TO POSTSECONDARY SCHOOLS?

As an individual with disabilities, there are a few additional things you need to consider when applying to college. Here are a few of those things:

1. **Self-disclosure**: Unlike in a K–12 school, where the special education teachers helped to make sure your teachers knew how to accommodate your disability so you could succeed in school, you now have to be your own advocate. The college will not ask you if you have a disability. You will need to find the office of disability services to tell them or self-disclose your disability and ask for accommodations, if needed. They will need you to show them an assessment documenting your disability. If you do not choose to identify as a person with a disability or if that disability will not impact your college classes, you will be expected to meet all the requirements in the same way other students do, without accommodations or supports. You need to make this decision in the beginning. If you do poorly in a class, you cannot go back to ask for accommodations for work that was previously done.

2. **Disability documentation**: If you want accommodations, you will need to provide documentation of your disability to the college's disability services office. This documentation typically includes a diagnosis from a qualified professional, as well as an explanation of how the disability impacts you in the academic environment.

3. **Accommodations request**: If you self-disclose and provide documentation of your disability, you can request accommodations to support your learning needs during the application process and throughout your college education. Common accommodations include extended testing time, audio versions of textbooks, and note-takers.

4. **Accessible application materials**: If you have a documented disability, you can request accessible application materials and accommodations to the application process.

5. **Disability services office**: Most colleges have a disability services office or center that provides support and accommodations for students with disabilities. It's important that you connect with this office early in the application process to discuss your needs and

learn about available services. Also, keep in mind that accommodations usually cannot be instantly put in place. They may take time. For example, if you need a note-taker, it may take the disability services officer time to locate a student in your course who is willing to take on that responsibility.

6. **Individualized education plan (IEP) or 504 plan**: If you have an IEP or 504 plan from high school, talk with the college's disability services officer about the accommodations you had in the past and your transition plan. Colleges may require updated documentation or assessments to determine appropriate accommodations in a college setting.

7. **Accessible housing**: If you plan to live on campus and need accessible housing, you will need to communicate this in advance. Colleges typically provide accommodations such as wheelchair-accessible rooms, assistive devices, and support services for students living in residence halls or campus apartments.

8. **Transition programs**: Some colleges offer transition programs or support services specifically designed for students with disabilities. Your college may provide peer mentors or academic coaching. They may also provide specialized workshops on topics like self-advocacy or disability rights.

9. **Financial aid and scholarships**: Students with disabilities may be eligible for specific types of financial assistance. Your OVR (Office of Vocational Rehabilitation) can help you to find out about these opportunities.

10. **Support services**: In addition to academic accommodations, your school may offer services that will help to ensure your success in the college environment, so it is good to find out about these early in your college experience. Many schools offer free counseling, health services, career guidance, tutoring, and assistive technology labs to help students with disabilities succeed academically and transition to employment or further education.

Applying to college is a complex process for most students, but, as a student with disabilities, you have even more to think about! Knowing your rights and responsibilities under the disability laws and communicating clearly are key. You will need to be proactive in advocating for the necessary accommodations and support services to ensure a successful college experience. Colleges are committed to their students' success! Look to those in the college community as partners in the process of helping you to achieve your goals.

RESOURCES

Kelley, K., Mattis, J., & Parsley, M. (2019). Managing the admission process at college programs for students with ID. Think College Resource Library. https://thinkcollege.net/resource/admissions/managing-the-admissions-process-at-college-programs-for-students-with-id
Office of Special Education and Rehabilitative Services. (2020, August). *A transition guide to postsecondary education for students and youth with disabilities.* https://sites.ed.gov/idea/idea-files/policy-guidance-transition-guide-postsecondary-education-employment-students-youth-disabilities-august-2020/#:~:text=While%20permission%20to%20reprint%20this,Washington%2C%20D.C.%2C%202020%202020

COMPLETING THE COLLEGE APPLICATION

The purpose of a college application is for the college to determine whether or not an applicant is a good fit for the institution. All schools want their students to be successful! Some schools are able to accept most of the students who apply. Less competitive schools, particularly community colleges, may have open admissions, but students take placement exams to determine whether or not they are ready for the coursework in their program. Those who are underprepared are given the opportunity to take remedial classes in basic skills, such as reading, writing, or math, before pursuing credit-bearing courses in their program.

Other schools have competitive admissions due to the limited number of students they can take. Very competitive schools may look for outstanding ability in a particular area. They may also look beyond grades and academic ability. Depending on the mission of the university and the program goals, a school may look for evidence of leadership skills or dedication to serving the community. They may look for involvement in extracurricular activities or a record of volunteer work.

Here's an overview of the kinds of information most applications include:

1. **Personal information**: The application begins with basic personal information. In addition to your name and address, you will need to provide your email address and phone number so the

school can contact you easily. (Be sure you check your email and phone messages regularly once you apply, in case the school needs to contact you.) You will also need to include your birth date and citizenship status. This basic contact information is used to create a file for the applicant and to facilitate communication during the application process. In addition, if the student is accepted, the personal information becomes a part of the student's permanent record at the institution.

2. **Educational background**: The school will want to know about your previous education. This includes your high school and any other schools you have attended following high school graduation. Even if you have just taken one course, you should include that school on the application. The college will most likely need the name and location, your graduation date, and your grade point average (GPA). Competitive schools may ask for your class rank. This is where you fall in terms of the grade point averages of everyone in the class.

3. **Standardized test scores**: If a college requires standardized test scores, they may ask you to self-report your scores in addition to having the official score reports sent directly from the testing agency to the school. Standardized test scores help the school predict the likelihood of your ability to succeed in college-level courses.

4. **Academic history and coursework**: Though most schools require transcripts of your previous courses, some applications may ask you to list the courses you took in high school or at other institutions. You should be sure to mention if any were honors, advanced placement (AP), or dual enrollment (college-level courses taken during high school) courses. If you have taken AP or dual enrollment courses, you may not have to take some of the courses typically required for students during the first two years of the program. In this section, you may also see a place to list awards you received during high school or in schools attended after graduation.

5. **Extracurricular activities**: Colleges care about more than academics! They will want to know about your involvement in extracurricular activities. This can include clubs, sports, volunteer work, internships, or jobs. You will probably need to include the dates of your participation in each activity and any leadership roles or offices you held. This part of the application helps the admissions

team gain a sense of your fit within the college community, including your potential for leadership and participation in athletics.

6. **Essays or personal statements**: Many colleges require applicants to write essays or personal statements as part of the application process. This is your chance to showcase your personality and the unique contribution you can make to the school community. The prompts may vary, and it is important to address exactly what the prompts specify. So, for example, if the essay prompt asks you to describe a specific challenge and how you have overcome it, don't write about your passion for biology! Faith-based institutions may be looking for applicants whose personal and religious beliefs align with those of the school.

7. **Letters of recommendation**: Most schools ask for letters of recommendation. Choose people who are not related to you and who can speak to your ability to succeed in the college setting. The application may specify the people you should seek recommendations from. For example, you may need one recommendation from a teacher or counselor and one from a job supervisor or coach. The application may request contact information for your recommenders so they can be sent electronic forms to complete. Be sure the contact information you provide is accurate, and request permission to include the person as a recommender before submitting his or her name.

8. **Supplemental materials**: Depending on the college and program, you may be asked to submit supplemental materials such as a portfolio (for art or design programs), audition tapes (for performing arts programs), writing samples, or additional information requested by the college.

9. **Application fee**: Most colleges require an application fee when you submit the application. However, those with demonstrated financial need can often have the fee waived.

10. **Optional interviews**: Some colleges offer optional interviews as part of the application process. You may find an interview to be to your advantage, especially if your previous academic performance was weak. The interview gives you a chance to explain any challenges you had to overcome or extenuating circumstances that impacted your performance. The interview also gives you the opportunity to bring a portfolio that can serve as a prompt to showcase special experiences like volunteer work, personal

interests, abilities, and the like. You may even request permission to show brief video clips to demonstrate your skills and expertise.

11. **Declaration of major or program of interest**: Most applications will ask you to list your intended major. Some colleges allow students to apply as undecided or explore different academic options during their first year. However, deciding on a major early in the college experience helps to ensure that the student makes the best use of their time and money by not taking courses they do not need for their program.

12. **Parent or guardian information**: Applicants may need to provide information about their parents or guardians, including their names, occupations, education levels, and contact information. Information about parents may seem like an odd and perhaps unfair question to ask on an application! However, such information is often used by the university for federal reporting purposes. The university may have to report information, such as the socioeconomic status of their applicants, to demonstrate equity in their admissions processes. The information can also help the university understand the kinds of services and support that will benefit its student population.

This site provides a college application worksheet: https://www.acenet.edu/Documents/College%20Application%20Worksheet%20final.pdf. Though you may not need all of the information on this worksheet for every application, completing this worksheet will help you to consider the kinds of information you are likely to need, and it will enable you to complete applications more efficiently and accurately.

Tip: After reading about applications and the kinds of information required, look up the websites for several schools you think you may be interested in. Compare the applications for the schools. What questions do all of the schools ask? Are there any questions or application materials that are unique to specific schools? Why do you think they may ask for that information?

COMMON APPLICATION OR "COMMON APP"

Many prospective college students are unaware of the "Common App." This is a standardized application that allows you to use one application to apply to many different schools. This is a great time-saver! Not all schools accept the Common App, but since more than 700 do, it's worth checking. ("Common App;" n.d. commonapp.org.)

Here are key features and aspects of the Common Application:

1. **Single application form**: The applicant saves time and money by completing one application that can be used for multiple schools.
2. **Member colleges and universities**: The Common App is accepted by more than 700 colleges and universities, including public and private schools.
3. **Application components**: The Common App includes all of the typical components required on most college applications.
4. **Essay prompts**: The Common App provides a set of essay prompts that applicants can choose from.
5. **Application fee waiver**: Most colleges require a fee for each application submitted. This can add up quickly for students who apply to several colleges! Students who have financial need can request an application fee waiver through the Common App. This can help to provide access to college for a greater number of students.
6. **Recommendation letters**: The Common App simplifies the process of requesting recommendations and having recommenders send their letters to multiple places. The applicant can request recommendation letters through the app, the letter can be submitted, and the applicant can track whether or not letters have been submitted.
7. **Application dashboard**: An application dashboard allows the applicant to track and manage all of their application materials. The dashboard makes it easy to be aware of deadlines by setting notifications and reminders.

Some colleges that accept the Common App may have additional admission requirements like supplemental questions to answer or materials to submit. For example, admission to an art program may require the submission of a portfolio. Admission to a music program may require a recording of the student's performance. But, overall, the Common App greatly simplifies the application process.

THE ADMISSIONS ESSAY

Grades and test scores don't tell the whole story! Perhaps you have been concerned that you will be denied admission to the school of your choice because of your high school grades. The essay can be your chance to give the admissions committee a more complete picture of who you are and what you can add to the school community. The essay can help to reveal your personality, values, goals, experiences, and unique qualities, while also providing you with an opportunity to explain any extenuating circumstances that may have impacted your past academic performance.

Tip: The essay can be a great opportunity to explain the circumstances of past academic performance but be careful not to make excuses. For example, if a move from one school to another caused you to have some gaps in your knowledge when you began at your new school, that is an understandable explanation for a drop in grades. However, complaining that the teacher didn't like you, so he gave you a poor grade, is an excuse that makes it sound like you don't take responsibility for your academic performance.

The essay demonstrates your writing ability and critical thinking skills, and it provides some insight into your personality and work ethic. All of these are important components of success in the college environment. What admissions committees focus on when they review essays will vary, depending on the nature of the school and the type of student they hope to attract. The prompt will give you some clues about what the school values. For example, suppose you are given the following prompt: *Describe your long-term career goals and aspirations. How do you envision using your education to make a difference?* The school likely wants to attract students who are passionate about their chosen field and who demonstrate a desire to impact society through service. In this case, being clear about your career path and how your education will help you achieve your life goals, as well as highlighting ways you have engaged in service to your community, can help to make your essay stand out.

Some of the things the admissions committee may consider as they review your essay and some questions you can ask yourself as you plan are included in table 4.1 on page 73.

Tip: Since many colleges no longer require standardized test scores, the admissions essay is, in many cases, more important than it used to be. Be sure to proofread your essay carefully and give yourself enough time to review it and make changes. First, let your essay "cool" after writing it. In other words, give yourself a day or so after writing to come back and take

Table 4.1 The Admissions Essay: What Do They Really Want to Know?

What the Essay Reveals	Questions to Ask Yourself
Your approach to the prompt	Did you answer the question directly and completely?
Enthusiasm and areas of interest	Read your essay aloud. Do you sound enthusiastic about continuing your education? Are you passionate about your career path? Do you have well-rounded interests?
Personal experiences	What unique personal experiences have you had? What kinds of experiences have shaped you into the person you are today? What challenges have you overcome?
Goals	Has the prompt asked for personal or career goals or both? What goals do you have for your personal growth? What are your long-term career goals?
Evidence of maturity and growth	Does your essay explain rather than make excuses for past performance? Do you show how you have grown through the challenges you have experienced?
Leadership potential	Have you explained situations when you demonstrated the ability to positively influence others and/or work together toward a common goal?
Personality of the applicant	What are your best personality traits? Would someone reading the application gain a sense of what you are like, rather than just what you have done or hope to accomplish? Would a reader of the application have a sense of how you would fit into the campus community?
Organization of ideas	Is the presentation of your ideas logical? Have you structured paragraphs well, with one main idea per paragraph?
Clarity of expression	Ask someone else to read your essay. Are there parts they don't understand?
Sentence structure and word choice	Have you avoided sentence-level errors, such as incorrect subject-verb agreement, run-on sentences, and sentence fragments? Have you used a variety of sentence types? Are your word choices appropriate?
Proper spelling and use of punctuation and other mechanics of writing	Have you proofread your essay for spelling, punctuation, and other errors?
Adherence to directions	Have you followed the directions for the prompt? Are you within the required word limit?

a fresh look. Read it aloud so you can hear how it sounds. This may help you to catch some places where your ideas don't flow, or your organization doesn't make sense. Then, beginning with the last sentence in your essay and moving toward the first, read each sentence aloud once again. This will help you to catch sentence-level errors and awkward wording. Finally, have someone else proofread your essay for you.

SAMPLE ADMISSIONS ESSAY

The following essay is a sample response to the following prompt: "Write a 250-word essay that describes a significant experience, achievement, or challenge and its impact on you."

Growing up with a physical disability has been a defining aspect of my life, shaping my experiences, perspectives, and resilience. One significant challenge I faced was learning to navigate a world not always designed with accessibility in mind. From early childhood, simple tasks like climbing stairs or accessing public spaces required innovative solutions and adaptations.

This challenge became an opportunity for growth and empowerment. I learned to advocate for myself, speak up for accessibility rights, and educate others about the importance of inclusive design. Through this journey, I discovered a passion for disability advocacy and accessibility awareness.

One particular achievement stands out in my mind. During high school, I spearheaded a campaign to improve accessibility on campus. I collaborated with school administrators, fellow students, and community organizations to identify barriers and implement solutions. From installing ramps and accessible restrooms to raising awareness about invisible disabilities, our efforts made a tangible difference in the lives of students with disabilities.

This experience not only enhanced accessibility but also fostered a sense of belonging and inclusion for all students. It taught me the power of collective action and the impact of advocacy on creating positive change.

Ultimately, overcoming challenges related to my disability has shaped my character, instilled perseverance, and fueled my determination to create a more inclusive and accessible world. This journey has deeply impacted me, igniting a lifelong commitment to advocacy, empowerment, and breaking barriers for individuals with disabilities.

RESOURCES

"The Common App." https://www.commonapp.org/

Winthrop Think College Application for 2023/24 Academic Year: https://www .winthrop.edu/uploadedFiles/ceshs/winthroplife/Winthrop-Think-College -Application.pdf

IPSE RESOURCES

APPENDIX A: PROFILE OF GRADUATE STUDENTS

INDEPENDENT LIVING

- I communicate with course instructors, job supervisors, and others both in person and via phone or email.
- I access and correspond via email.
- I am involved in activities and events in my community/on my campus.
- I travel safely and efficiently around campus and town.
- I budget money to allow for saving, spending, and giving.
- I maintain healthy personal hygiene by showering, brushing teeth, and washing clothes.
- I maintain a healthy living space by cleaning my room.
- I exercise on a regular basis.
- I make healthy eating choices daily.
- I prepare healthy meals on my own.

COURSEWORK

- I attend class in accordance with the university attendance policy.
- I request accommodations/modifications in a timely manner.
- I attend my scheduled mentor sessions.
- I email my professor about my strengths and needs.
- I access online platforms for coursework and assignments.

EMPLOYABILITY

- I have an interest and desire to work.
- I can identify one to three career interests.
- I can secure a job by applying, submitting a résumé, and interviewing.
- I have soft skills such as: punctuality, dependability, positive attitude, time management, poise, persistence, and enthusiasm
- I can produce vital information for an application including: my address, contact info, and references.

APPENDIX B: SUGGESTED SKILLS FOR
SC IPSE STUDENT SUCCESS

This document is for parents, students, teachers, transition specialists, and related service providers. Highlighted are the six domains that college programs across the state are focused on as it relates to preparing your child, student, consumer for successful post-school outcomes.

Across these outlined domains, SC IPSE programs offer differing levels of support, but basic knowledge and ability to practice these skills are foundational for a successful experience. Of most importance, students should have *self-determination* and a *desire* to attend college!

ACADEMICS

- Ability to effectively communicate with course instructors and academic coaches
- Ability to access and effectively correspond using email
- Ability to take notes (via whatever communication mode works best for individual)
- Ability to navigate online platforms for course assignments
- Ability to ask for support when needed

CAREER DEVELOPMENT

- Demonstrates an interest and desire to work
- Ability to identify one to three career interests
- Ability to identify the basic requirements for securing a job (résumé, cover letter, interview)
- Demonstrates soft skills such as communication, teamwork, flexibility, time management, patience, decision-making, problem-solving, positive attitude, and dependability

INDEPENDENT LIVING

- Ability to practice appropriate hygiene care
- Ability to practice healthy eating and lifestyle habits
- Ability to perform housekeeping duties (keeping a living space clean, laundry)
- Ability to practice money management
- Awareness of and interest in various modes of transportation and navigation

PERSONAL WELLNESS

- Ability to identify and express emotions in various situations
- Ability to self-advocate and request help when needed
- Identify support team members who can help during challenges
- Ability to identify and manage stressors
- Ability to identify and practice healthy habits for maintaining physical, mental, and emotional well-being

SOCIALIZATION

- Appropriate use of assistive technology (including knowing which applications and platforms to have access to and how to use them. Examples include speech-to-text or voice recognition)
- Initiates campus involvement (joining campus clubs and organizations)
- Interest in community involvement (volunteer and service opportunities)
- Demonstrates an interest in meeting new people and making friends/establishing relationships

GENERAL SKILLS

- Time management (setting and following alarms and schedules)
- Knowledge of personal identification (name, address, phone number, disability, and medical conditions)
- Awareness of personal safety (safely crossing streets, locking doors, and keeping belongings safe)
- Awareness of assistive technologies and devices that are required to help him or her thrive (mobility aids, hearing/sight aids, adaptive equipment, etc.)

Additional Resources

Think College provides resources, technical assistance, and training related to college options for students with intellectual disability and manages the only national listing of college programs for students with intellectual disability in the United States. Several of their resources are specific to preparing for the college experience.

- Think College Tips for IEP Teams (http://thinkcollege.net/sites /default/files/files/resources/TCPub_Tips_for_IEP_Teams_Pacer .pdf)
- Think College Foundational Skills for College and Career Learning Plan (http://thinkcollege.net/sites/default/files/files/resources/ foundation%20skills%207_6_17mbdt.pdf)
- Think College Postsecondary Education Expectations (http:// thinkcollege.net/sites/default/files/files/college_expectation_sec ondary_preparation.pdf)

APPENDIX C: K–12 TRANSITION ROAD MAP: BEGINNING WITH IPSE IN MIND

This document was designed for educators, parents, students with intellectual and developmental disability, and related service providers. The following blocks highlight skills and action steps to take across the lifespan as postsecondary opportunities and outcomes are considered. Promoting high expectations, practicing inclusion, and fostering independence at each stage will maximize preparedness.

ELEMENTARY SCHOOL YEARS (K–5)

- **IEP**: The team should establish baselines across academic and functional domains and develop appropriate goals and support. Discuss IPSE as a long-term goal and begin talking about college with the student so they are aware of options.
- **Curriculum**: Evaluation and assessment should be conducted to help determine learning, adaptive, and related difficulties that may impact child's experience.
- **Skills**: Focus should be placed on age-appropriate tasks, such as direction and rule following, and simple routines.
- **Activities of daily living**: Tasks such as identifying and understanding emotions, basic responsibility, active listening, and effective communication should be highlighted.

Reach out to Family Connections (www.familyconnectionsc.org) of South Carolina to learn about the resources available to families at each stage of life. Explore Charting the LifeCourse (www.lifecoursetools .com) for early and ongoing transition planning.

MIDDLE SCHOOL YEARS (6–8)

- **IEP**: The team should continue to create academic and functional goals, and the student should be primary in the conversation. At age 13, transition plans are a required part of the IEP.
- **Curriculum**: Students should be on an academic track that suits their learning needs and supports their long-term success. Transition interests should be explored through inventories and surveys.
- **Skills**: Focus should be placed on identifying personal and career likes and strengths.
- **Activities of daily living**: Tasks such as self-care and proper hygiene, creating and following a schedule, managing time and money, and independent choice-making should be practiced.

Establish a case with South Carolina Vocational Rehabilitation (http://sc-scvrd.civicplus.com/217/Find-My-Area-Office) as a consumer to gain access to their transition services and supports. Make note of and contact the following agencies for additional supports: AbleSC (www.able-sc.org); DDSN (https://transitionta.org/postsecondary-education-training-prep); Disability Rights SC (www.disabilityrightssc.org); ARC SC (www.arcsc.org); Think College (https://thinkcollege.net).

HIGH SCHOOL YEARS (9–11)

- **IEP**: Begin thinking about what reasonable outcomes there are for the student and establish a graduation plan and track (diploma or non-diploma seeking). Let the student's self-determination drive the transition process as they explore educational, career, and independent living opportunities post high school. At age 18, transfer of rights enables the student to make legal decisions related to his or her IEP.
- **Curriculum**: Students should begin researching IPSE options, focus on volunteer and job experiences, explore career interests, and learn the process of applying for and acquiring a job.
- **Skills**: Focus should be placed on being well-versed on individual's identifying information, acquiring an ID/permit, and knowing health and medical history.

• **Activities of daily living**: Tasks such as self-determination, awareness on modes of transportation and how to access them, community involvement, and life away from home should be focused on. Emphasis should be placed on meal preparation and healthy living.

Continue seeking guidance from South Carolina Vocational Rehabilitation. Access the ThinkCollege College Search Tool (https:// thinkcollege.net/college-search?f[0]=tc_state_province%3ASouth%20 Carolina) to explore the programs across the United States. Visit SCIPSEC (https://scipsec.com) to gather more information about the six IPSEs in South Carolina!

SENIOR YEAR AND SUMMER BEFORE IPSE

• **IEP**: Begin thinking about what academic accommodations and supports might be needed to be successful in college, and how to advocate for and access them. Parents and corresponding professionals should review legal and financial processes and fulfilling related obligations. At age 22, individuals with intellectual or developmental disability are no longer eligible for a free and appropriate education (FAPE) under the Individuals with Disabilities Education Act (IDEA). All decisions and steps going forward are governed under the Americans with Disabilities Act (ADA).

• **Curriculum**: By the beginning of senior year, begin applying to IPSEs (most applications are open August to October). Make campus visits and take program tours of the IPSEs of interest.

• **Skills**: Students should know what it means to be self-determined and advocate for themselves. Students should be well-prepared to speak to professionals about their disability and the academic and functional accommodations most helpful to them.

• **Activities of daily living**: Tasks such as self-care and hygiene (including medication) and self-regulation should be practiced. Independent living tasks such as doing laundry, cleaning the house, following a schedule, and waking to an alarm are all great to prepare for life in college!

Additional Transition Resources

The **PACER Center** enhances the quality of life and expands opportunities for children, youth, and young adults with all disabilities and their families so each person can reach his or her highest potential.

- PACER's "Preparing for Postsecondary Education" (www.pacer .org/transition/learning-center/postsecondary/preparing-for-post secondary.asp)
- PACER'S "10 Tips to Help With Transition" (www.pacer.org/par ent/php/PHP-c107.pdf)
- PACER's "College Planning" (https://transitionta.org/postsecond ary-education-training-prep)

The National Technical Assistance Center on Transition (NTACT) provides technical assistance to all states and US territories to ensure transition-age youth with disabilities receive high-quality education services.

- NTACT "Postsecondary Education Toolkit" (https://transitionta .org/postsecondary-education-training-prep)

The National Resource Center for Supported Decision-Making (NRC-SDM) brings together various partners to ensure that input is obtained from all relevant stakeholder groups including older adults, people with intellectual and developmental disabilities (I/DD), family members, advocates, professionals, and providers as individuals with disabilities learn about their right(s) as it relates to exercising their power to make self-determined choices.

- "Supported Decision-Making Tools" (https://supporteddecisi onmaking.org/resource-library)

APPENDIX D: VIDEO INTERVIEW QUESTION EXAMPLES

Video Interview Questions

- What are some things you like doing on your own time (hobbies, activities)?

- Besides work and classes, what are some activities you would like to do at WCU?

- Do you believe you will succeed in college? If so, why do you think you will do well?

- Do you want to get a job after you leave college? If so, what job would you like to have?

- Do you want to live with your family after you leave college? If not, where would you like to live and what type of home would you like to live in (trailer, house, apartment, group home, etc.)?

APPENDIX E: WINTHROPLIFE APPLICANT
INTERVIEW QUESTIONS

Student: _____

Date: _____

WTC Applicant Interview

1. Why did you choose to apply to IPSE at Winthrop?

2. What are your goals for the program?

3. What are your plans after college?

4. What classes/activities do you enjoy?

5. What classes/activities would you like to take?

6. What type of job would you like?

7. Independence
   What chores do you complete?

   Have you worked?

   What do you do if you do not know something?

8. Safety
   Navigation:
   Health:
   Relationships:
   Money:

9. Time Management
   What do you do when you feel you do not have time?

   What would you do if you had to miss/be late for work?

10. Money Management
    Who manages your money now?

    Have you ever ordered at a restaurant and paid before?

    What would you do if you go to a restaurant with your friends and you do not have enough money to pay for your meal?

    Do you have online banking?

11. Social
    Where do you hang out with friends?

    What would you do if your roommate was playing loud music?

    What would you say if a stranger asked for your money?

12. Other

APPENDIX E: WINTHROPLIFE APPLICANT
INTERVIEW RUBRIC

Name: _____

Table 4.2   WinthropLIFE Applicant Interviews

	Proficient 6 Points	Emerging 3 Points	Beginning 0 Points
Choice to Apply to WinthropLIFE and Pursue IPSE	Provides a response that includes self-driven motives for wanting to pursue an IPSE at Winthrop.	Provides a response that is primarily driven by parents/guardians/teachers.	Does not have a clear reason for wanting to pursue IPSE.
Goals	Clearly outlines two goals that they have for themselves.	Clearly outlines one goal that they have for themselves. May require questioning prompts.	Is unable to provide a goal that they have for themselves, even with prompting.
Future Plans for Independent Living	Has clear goals/plans for living independently after college and/or has a desire to grow in the area of independent living skills.	Requires some prompting to identify plans for independent living or plans to live at home with parents.	Does not have a clear desire to grow in independent living skills.
Future Plans for Employment	Has clear goals for employability after college and is able to identify how that relates to WinthropLIFE.	Has vague goals for employability but does express an interest in obtaining employment after college.	Does not have a desire to work after college.
Hobbies/Interests	Is able to identify at least two hobbies/interests and shows definite excitement about involvement on campus	Has limited range of hobbies/interests and shows moderate excitement about involvement on campus.	Has limited range of hobbies/interests and shows minimal excitement about involvement on campus.

(Continued)

Table 4.2   (Continued)

	Proficient 6 Points	*Emerging* 3 Points	*Beginning* 0 Points
Present Levels	Is able to describe areas of strength and weakness, has experience with chores and responsibility, and shows an interest in improving skill levels.	Can describe areas of strength and weakness with some prompting, has some experience with independence and responsibility, and shows an interest in improving skill levels.	Shows limited interest in improving skill level and taking on more independence/ responsibility.
Problem-Solving	Is able to problem-solve when given scenarios with minimum prompting.	Is able to problem-solve when given scenarios with maximum prompting.	Is unable to problem-solve even with supports.
Receptive to Help	Applicant is friendly, personable, and willing to accept prompting/ support if needed.	Applicant is willing to accept prompting/ support if needed	Applicant becomes argumentative or is unwilling to accept prompting/support if needed.
Behavior	Applicant is able to sit and attend through the interview without maladaptive behaviors.	Applicant is able to sit and attend through the interview with minimum prompting for behaviors.	Applicant's behaviors are disruptive during the interview or applicant requires significant prompting during the interview.

Total: _____

APPENDIX F: I.C.E. CUBE FILLABLE AND EXAMPLE

Table 4.3　ICE Worksheet

_____'s I.C.E. Cube

Date _____

INDEPENDENT LIVING	COURSEWORK	EMPLOYABILITY
Present Levels:	Previous Courses:	Previous Employment/ Internship:
_____	1. _____	1. _____
_____	2. _____	2. _____
_____	3. _____	3. _____
_____	4. _____	Current: _____
	5. _____	
	6. _____	
	7. _____	Job Skills:
Short-Term Goals:	8. _____	1. _____
1. _____	9. _____	2. _____
2. _____	10. _____	3. _____
3. _____	11. _____	4. _____
	12. _____	5. _____
	13. _____	
	14. _____	
		Skills Development Goals:
		1. _____
		2. _____
Long-Term Goals:	Preferred Courses:	3. _____
1. _____	1. _____	
2. _____	2. _____	
3. _____	3. _____	Dream Job:
	4. _____	
	5. _____	1. _____
	6. _____	2. _____
	7. _____	3. _____

Table 4.4   Alex's I.C.E. Cube

INDEPENDENT LIVING	COURSEWORK	EMPLOYABILITY
Present Levels	**Previous Courses**	**Previous Employment/**
• Good hygiene	1. Weight training	**Internship**
• Fixes prepared meals	2. Religion 220	1. Kroger (bagger/returns)
• Relies on family/	3. Biology 150	2. Current: WU Cafeteria
friends for travel	4. Rock climbing	
• Cleans bathroom and	5. Intro to computers	**Job Skills**
makes bed	6. Racquetball	1. Punctual
• Dresses appropriately		2. Diligent
	Preferred Courses	3. Good appearance
Short-Term Goals	1. Dinosaurs	4. Follows rules
1. Healthy eating habits	2. Rock climbing	
2. Using public	3. Martial arts	**Skills Development Goals**
transportation	4. Art (pottery)	1. Communicate with
3. Personal grooming	5. Computer science	coworkers
	6. Disc golf	2. Computer and cash
Long-Term Goals		3. Multitasking
1. Driver's license		
2. Expressing self/		**Dream Job**
communication		1. Ross Warehouse
3. Budgeting/money		2. Stars and Strikes (arcade)
value		3. Landscape

5

HOW DO WE NAVIGATE
SUPPORT SERVICES?

The level of support and the types of services available to you will vary according to the type of program. In some cases, the support services must be set up with the appropriate office within the institution. This chapter will help you and your family anticipate the types of support services typically offered for each type of program and know the steps to take to connect with needed services.

Topics covered in this chapter include:

- services you typically encounter early in the process;
- services related to academics;
- out-of-class support services; and
- how to connect with needed services

You may think of college or vocational school as simply a place where you take the classes you need to prepare for the job you hope to have. But college is much more! The college environment is more like a community. The community you live in at home provides many different services needed by the people who live there, like hospitals, stores, gas stations, and restaurants. The college community provides many services needed by the students who attend. In this chapter, you will learn about the types of services you may find on the campus. Of course, there are differences in the services provided by different types of schools, but this chapter will introduce you to services that are commonly found within college communities.

Tip: When you visit colleges, use the campus map to look for the offices where these services are found.

ADMISSIONS OFFICE

The admissions office will likely be the first point of contact you have with a college or university, and they will communicate with you from the time you express interest in the school through the time when you receive a decision letter. Most colleges appoint a specific admissions counselor to each applicant when they make contact with the school. The admissions counselor can be an excellent resource as you go through the admissions process. If you have questions or concerns as you prepare your application materials, contact your admissions counselor. If they cannot answer your question, they can direct you to the proper person or department. The admissions office works closely with other departments in the school, so they can help you with questions about things such as the requirements of the program you are interested in, financial aid, and athletics.

The admissions office has many responsibilities, but their primary focus is recruiting students and supporting them through the admissions process. Colleges aim to attract a diverse student body that will be a good fit for the school community. They also plan events, such as open houses and orientations. An open house can be a good way to see the campus and learn more about the program you are interested in.

REGISTRAR'S OFFICE

The registrar's office keeps records of all classes you register for and complete. This office ensures that you have taken all of the courses required for the degree or credential you receive. They also enforce policies regarding registration for courses. For example, if a course requires you to complete an entry-level course first, they may not allow you to take the course you tried to register for. This office also sets deadlines and procedures for registering for and withdrawing from courses. If you decide not to take a course you have registered for, you cannot simply stop attending. You must go through the school's procedure for withdrawal from a course. Also, refunds are usually only given for a certain period of time during the semester. It's important to know the deadline for getting your money back if you decide not to take the course.

The registrar's office also tracks the grades you receive for each course. When you graduate, you may need a transcript, which is a record of all of the courses you have taken, the grades you received, your overall grade point average (GPA), and the degree or certificate you earned.

FINANCIAL AID OFFICE

Your college financial aid office will prepare a specific financial aid package for you by considering your personal circumstances. As mentioned in earlier chapters, you must complete the FAFSA form (Free Application for Federal Student Aid reviewed in chapter 3) to receive any sort of aid. The financial aid package may include loans, scholarships, grants, and/or work study eligibility. You should be informed of the contents of your financial aid package before you decide to attend any college so that you have all the information needed to make an informed decision for you and your family. This office works closely with the admissions staff and the office where you pay your bill. The office where you make payments can be called by different names, such as the bursar, the cashier, or student accounts office.

As an individual with disabilities, the financial aid department may play an important role in your college experience. Here are some ways they can help:

1. **Understanding**: Financial aid staff can provide you with information and support to understand the process to apply for funding to pay for college.
2. **Financial package**: Financial aid staff can provide you with information and support to understand your individualized financial aid package. What your financial aid package does not cover is also extremely important to be aware of. Colleges provide what is called a *net price calculator* to help estimate how much you will have to pay out of your own or your family's pocket.
3. **Knowledge**: The financial aid staff have a lot of knowledge that can assist students with understanding their own aid package. If your circumstances change after starting college, such as your parent losing his or her job, the staff can help guide you, as there may be more aid you can apply for.

ACADEMIC ADVISORS

One of the most important people you will meet on your college journey is your academic advisor. The academic advisor is usually a faculty member in the department of your college major. However, in some schools, other staff members advise students. The primary role of the academic advisor is to help you develop an academic plan to complete your program goal.

Your advisor knows the courses that are needed to meet the requirements of your program and when they are offered. Sometimes courses have to be taken in a certain order. Your advisor will help you select courses in the right sequence.

Your advisor will want to know about your career goals, how many classes you plan to take at one time, and what kinds of outside responsibilities you have. Though it is your choice whether or not to disclose your disability, the more information you give your academic advisor, the more they can help you create a plan that sets you up for success.

Most colleges have a designated period of time when registration for the following semester opens. During this time, you make an appointment to meet with your advisor. He or she will help you to select the courses you need and to understand the process your school uses to register for them. Some courses are more difficult to get into, as they fill up quickly and class size is limited. Registering as soon as registration opens can help you to get into the courses you need, when you need them.

You might think of your advisor as a mentor and support person. They can help you work through problems you may encounter in your courses. For example, suppose you have a professor that you think graded you too harshly on an assignment. You might go to your academic advisor for advice on how to work through that issue. You can also consult your advisor about how to connect with support services on campus or how to prepare for internships or job opportunities.

As an individual with disabilities, your advisor plays an especially important role. Here are some ways they can help:

1. **Navigating support services**: They guide students in accessing support services available on campus, such as disability services offices, tutoring centers, counseling services, and assistive technology resources.
2. **Advocacy**: Advisors can serve as advocates for students with disabilities, ensuring that they receive appropriate accommodations and support throughout their academic journey. They may also facilitate communication between students, faculty, and support services.
3. **Monitoring progress**: Advisors monitor students' academic progress and offer ongoing support and guidance. They may help students address any challenges they encounter and adjust their academic plans, as needed.

4. **Referrals**: If necessary, advisors can refer students to external resources and professionals, such as counselors, therapists, or medical specialists, to address additional needs related to their disabilities.

Overall, academic advisors play a key role in creating a supportive and inclusive environment for college students with disabilities, helping them navigate challenges and achieve their academic goals.

TUTORING AND WRITING CENTERS

Tutoring and writing centers are available to provide support to help students succeed in their courses. Sometimes schools have one center that provides both tutoring and writing help. In larger schools the centers may be separate.

Do you think tutoring is just for students who are struggling or failing? Not so! Tutoring and writing centers are available to provide academic support for *all* students. Many centers offer workshops on topics such as how to write a thesis statement, how to avoid plagiarism, and how to prepare for a test. They also offer one-on-one tutoring with a staff member or peer mentor. If you are working on an assignment for a particular class, the center may even try to match you with a tutor who has taken that particular class before. You can request help for specific assignments or more general help on study strategies for a topic in your course.

Sometimes tutors are in short supply. It can be a good idea to sign up for a tutor early in the semester. The center may have policies about attendance of scheduled tutoring sessions. If you cannot make a session, be sure to notify the center so your time slot can be offered to someone else.

Often, tutoring and writing centers staff work closely with staff from the college's office of disability services. The center may provide assistive technology and a location for alternative testing arrangements.

As a student with disabilities, here are some of the ways the tutoring and writing centers can help you:

1. **Academic support**: The centers provide tutoring to help you succeed in your courses.
2. **Emotional support**: If you are worried about a particular assignment or are struggling with content in your courses, the center staff can help to alleviate your anxiety by helping you interpret the

expectations for the assignment and developing a plan to manage the work you will need to complete.

3. **Workshops**: Check the schedule for workshops on a variety of topics. Even if you think you know about that topic, the presenters often provide tips that will help you to perform at your best.

4. **Assistive technology**: The centers often provide assistive technology.

5. **Alternative testing**: Working in conjunction with disability services, alternative testing is often provided through the tutoring center.

LIBRARY

You may think of the library as simply a place to find books, but college libraries offer many additional resources and services. They provide electronic databases with access to online journals, magazines, and e-books. If you attend a larger university, the library may provide access to special collections, like rare books or artwork. They may also provide technology devices. Sometimes the library offers workshops to help students better understand how to use the library resources. They may also host special speakers and other events.

You will need to become familiar with the resources provided by your school's library in order to succeed in writing papers and completing assignments. The librarians are always more than willing to assist students with locating and utilizing resources. If you need help, just ask! Librarians are there to assist students, and they are usually more than willing to do so. Most college libraries have a web page with links that may allow you to reserve books, access the databases, and request help.

The library can be an excellent place to study, either by yourself or with peers. Most libraries provide quiet study areas, some of which you can reserve, as well as places partners or groups can meet to work together on assignments. If you have a noisy roommate or if you find yourself easily distracted, the library may be key to your success!

As an individual with a disability, the library can help you in these ways:

1. **Research support**: Librarians will help you to locate resources you may not have thought of. In addition, they can help you learn to use the databases and search for the information you need. And,

if you are just overwhelmed and don't know where to begin with your research assignment, librarians can help you to get started.

2. **Study space**: Whether you need a quiet place to study or need to work with a partner or group, the library can be a good choice. You will find spaces for both in most libraries.

3. **Informational resources**: Many libraries publish their own resources to help students with their research for class assignments. You may find web-based resources on topics such as avoiding plagiarism and citing sources correctly.

OFFICE OF DISABILITY SERVICES

All colleges and universities have an office that provides services for individuals with disabilities. The name of this office may differ from school to school—for example, office of accessibility or office of disability services. By law, colleges must provide support services for individuals with disabilities who need accommodations. The Americans with Disabilities Act (ADA) ensures people with disabilities equal access and protects them against discrimination.

1. **Navigating support services**: College staff will not seek you out and evaluate you to determine if you are eligible for accommodations. Unlike K–12, individuals with disabilities need to "self-disclose" or tell their university they have a disability and provide an evaluation to document that disability. Once that documentation is provided, the student needs to set up an appointment with the office to determine the types of accommodations he or she will be provided. Generally, once this is determined, a letter is sent to each professor. It will be up to the student to talk with the professor about those accommodations.

2. **Types of accommodations**: College instructors should make course materials accessible following ADA (Americans with Disabilities Act) guidelines, which can include closed captioning, text-to-speech technology, and so on. Some of the additional individual accommodations might be extending deadlines for assignment submissions, taking tests in the testing center, using assistive technology, or having a sign language interpreter for class lectures. Your office for disability services will offer some common

accommodations, but don't be afraid to offer suggestions about what you need to do well in class.

3. **Advocacy**: You need to advocate for yourself by disclosing your disability to the office, meeting with staff to determine accommodations, and speaking with your professors about the needed accommodations. The office will also advocate for you if you report a violation of your accommodations or your inability to access spaces or services on campus.

STUDENT LIFE, STUDENT AFFAIRS, OR STUDENT EXPERIENCE

This is a division of the university made up of departments that support students in their out-of-class experiences. The staff that work in the student affairs division are typically experienced and educated on topics that relate to the ways in which college students develop. Therefore, student affairs staff are able to plan their departments' services and programs in a manner that directly supports student growth not only in providing a service for students in various ways but also in setting up opportunities for challenges that lead to the development of skills and maturity.

Specific departments within the overall student affairs division can vary among different colleges. Examples of departments within the division are student activities or engagement, leadership development, student conduct or judicial, counseling, wellness, diversity and equity, student health, identity (gender, sexuality, race, ethnic), orientation, first-year experience, housing and residence life, dean of students office, and sometimes athletics. Some of these departments will be addressed in the following pages.

As an individual with disabilities, some of the student affairs departments may play an important role in your college experience. Here are some ways they can help:

1. **Engagement and involvement**: Student affairs will provide many ways for you to get involved on campus. Staff know that students getting involved can lead to success in many ways such as stronger grades, higher satisfaction, degree completion, and career success. Involvement can take many forms such as joining a club or a sport; helping plan programs on campus; serving on student government or any leadership position; volunteering; participating

in a study group; having a campus job; and assisting with faculty research.

2. **Connection and sense of belonging**: Student affairs departments help students to connect to other people—from peers and friends to faculty, staff, alumni, and people in the community. Forming relationships helps students feel more connected to the campus community. Caring for others and being cared about helps remind students that they matter. Feeling a connection and a sense of belonging also makes college fun!

3. **Self-discovery**: Student affairs departments design services and programs that assist you in exploring what you like and do not like. Moreover, they can help you discover your passions. Discovering your passion can lead you to finding your purpose in life. You will also discover things that you're good at but never tried before. By engaging on campus, you will have opportunities to develop new skills. Engaging with the campus community can also result in developing confidence in yourself and a feeling of independence. It is important to note that self-growth and discovery can appropriately include failure, or you having to figure things out for yourself instead of someone doing it for you. You will not be handed a list of what you are passionate about. Instead, you must discover those things on your own, and student affairs helps set up opportunities for you to do that.

4. **Support and referral**: While no particular office will be able to answer every question you have, each will know whom to connect you with to provide the support that you need. As mentioned in chapter 2, the college's care team or behavioral intervention team is a clearinghouse of information designed for staff to assist students in striving for success, while trying not to allow any students to fall through the cracks.

DEAN OF STUDENTS

The dean of students is a resource available at the vast majority of colleges and universities that you can utilize when you aren't sure where to go for help. The dean's job is to help make connections between you and the departments and services your college provides. The dean is an advocate for students and helps them navigate policy, as well as providing support services. In addition, the dean of students typically supervises the college's conduct (judicial) system. The dean supervises several student affairs departments and is usually the second-in-command of the division, after the vice president. *Note*: your college may also have academic deans who work with the faculty and academic departments. Your first resource will usually be the dean of students rather than the academic dean.

As an individual with disabilities, your dean of students may play a role in helping you connect with resources. Here are some ways he or she can help:

1. **Advocate**: The dean of students' job involves knowing what students need and want. That information helps to inform planning of programming with other departments, as well as informs overall policy development that impacts students.
2. **Resource**: The dean of students assists in connecting students to required educational programs, such as required alcohol or consent programming or voter registration information. The dean helps to inform students of university policy and all the support resources available to them. Providing support to students happens both proactively, before anything bad happens, and reactively, as a follow up to something negative happening.
3. **Accountability**: The dean of students is usually responsible for the university's student conduct process. He or she helps students learn about and understand the university's expectations of students. They ensure that the process to hold students accountable is educational, assisting students in their learning and growth.
4. **Support and referral**: Students having major challenges typically work with the dean of students to coordinate support. The dean is the chair of the care team or behavioral intervention team and leads the effort, with many other departments, to reach out to students who are behaving in ways that cause others to be concerned about them.

HOUSING AND RESIDENCE LIFE

Living on campus involves more than simply a place to sleep and keep your belongings. It is a place where a strong sense of community is the perfect foundation for your growth and development. It is also a laboratory to experiment with the interpersonal skills needed for future jobs. It is an ideal place to develop independence and lasting friendships.

The "housing" part of "housing and residence life" refers to the physical operations of the department. Housing maintains buildings with upkeep and utilities, such as water, electricity, and heat. They help provide safe rooms, furniture, bathrooms, laundry facilities, and internet. They also help provide access to buildings and individual rooms through a key or access card system. Housing also employs staff to fix things that break throughout the year.

The "residence life" part of the department refers to the programming and the people who intentionally develop a sense of campus community. Staff are in their jobs because they deeply care about students and their success. Their goal is to provide an environment that is safe, functional, and healthy for all students.

Living on campus results in a separate charge to your bill, in addition to tuition. The living space expenses are referred to as "room." "Board" is often another charge that covers a meal plan. Most first-year students are required to purchase a meal plan while living on campus.

As an individual with disabilities, housing and residence life will play a very important role if you decide to live on campus. Here are some ways they can help:

1. **Housing**: Of course, the main purpose of this department is to provide safe, comfortable housing that supports studying and growth, with a focus on community. Colleges will often require students to live on campus their first year or two if they live further than an hour from campus. Those who live closer may have the option to live on or off campus. No college has an endless supply of private bathrooms, single rooms, or rooms on the first floor. Therefore, this department will have established procedures for any special room requests or accommodations. They can work with the disability services office to collaborate on possible needed paperwork and help communicate your needs. If you plan to live on campus, early connection with the housing and residence life staff is the best plan of action.

2. **Community development**: Full-time staff, as well as student staff, are in place to assist roommates in developing appropriate expectations of each other—this is sometimes referred to as a "roommate contract." Staff are there to assist if there are roommate problems that escalate. The staff sponsors programming in the residence halls that provides education on various topics and provides opportunities for residents to get to know each other and have fun

together. Depending on the style of housing (two double rooms that share a bathroom, apartment style, suites, or the traditional hallway of double rooms with one large, shared bathroom), staff will have different approaches to assisting residents with making friends. Anytime a student is having a hard time making friends, the resident assistant staff member can be a helpful resource.

3. **Community standards**: The housing and residence life department has policies and rules to follow, which are all part of learning to become an adult. There are rules that apply to building codes related to fire safety or the use of electrical appliances. There are rules that apply to laws and overall college policy. There are rules that apply to how to live with others, while balancing individual freedoms with respect for others to create a harmonious environment.

4. **Support**: Student staff members will live in the building among the students, typically referred to as resident assistants (RAs). Student staff are available much of the time to students in need. Most likely, there will also be a full-time staff member that lives in the building with you, referred to as a hall or resident director (RD). The staff participate in an on-call rotation so that at any time of the day or night, there is a housing and residence life staff member available for emergencies (in addition to campus safety/campus police staff).

HEALTH AND WELLNESS CENTER SERVICES

Most colleges have some sort of small medical center on campus to assist students by treating colds and other minor illnesses, providing specialist referrals, and administering injections such as the flu shot. They can be in communication with your doctor to provide more streamlined care. These offices are oftentimes referred to as the health center or wellness center. Services in the centers vary widely. Some function as urgent care clinics, while others only offer minimal services. Some are "free" (fees are included in your tuition) and some utilize your health insurance. Be sure to meet with your health and wellness center staff to gain a thorough understanding of what they do and do not offer. Here are some of the services that may be available through a health and wellness center:

1. **Health services**: In nonemergencies, health services can be your first stop when you are not feeling well or get injured. They will have any level of medical professional there to help you. Some centers have a combination of nurses, physician assistants, nurse practitioners, or doctors to treat you. For extreme emergencies, however, skip health services and call 911 directly or campus police to contact them on your behalf. In such cases, health services staff will likely be alerted and will arrive to assist.

2. **Wellness services**: Wellness means maintaining proactive behaviors that are good for you. This office may provide stress-relief programs, mindfulness programs, or weight loss support.

3. **Counseling services**: Some colleges have combined all departments that address health of any kind into one department. Counseling services are sometimes included. (See page 106).

4. **Education**: This department will most likely try to educate students on how to stay healthy or how to treat minor illnesses. Some campuses train student leaders who are dedicated to teaching other students about health topics. Those student leaders can be called peer educators.

5. **Collaboration and referral**: Health services may collaborate with your doctor to continue treatments that you were previously prescribed. Staff may also work with other college departments to help provide focused care; such may be the case with concussion care for student athletes or counseling for a student with disordered eating. Separately, if a serious illness or injury is suspected after a visit, the staff can connect you to more specialized care.

CAMPUS POLICE

All colleges have a campus police or security department. In some colleges, they are also sworn police officers with the town or city that the college is located within. In this case, some are armed and have the power to make arrests. At other colleges, the staff in this department are not sworn officers with the local police force but, rather, report only to the college administration. In either case, they are the main point of contact to get help in the case of an extreme emergency or to report a crime.

Campus police staff will typically move around campus continuously. They will have a presence at large events. They will assist with traffic control, especially on days when large-scale events occur on campus. Some residence halls will have a campus police officer staff the front desk, controlling access to the building. The campus police staff are responsible for reporting crimes covered under the Clery Act, a law focused on making students aware of how safe a campus is and what events students should be aware of. They will monitor campus emergency call boxes or any emergency apps made available to students and may monitor parking lots or specific parts of campus.

As an individual with disabilities, the campus police department may play an important role during your time in college. Here are some ways they can help:

1. **Safety**: Campus police staff will take reports and investigate crimes that take place on campus. They will work with college administration to try to correct anything on campus that is not safe or is a hazard. Therefore, you can report any potential hazards you notice to campus police.
2. **Operations**: Operations includes parking, fire safety, overall policy enforcement, work with the physical plant department, and the campus ID system, including access to buildings.
3. **Education:** Watch for notices to participate in programs about topics such as self-defense courses or theft reduction.
4. **Emergency support**: If a student is hurt, campus police are quick responders. For on-campus emergencies, it is typically faster to call campus police for assistance because they know campus well, while the town or city police may easily get lost. This can cost precious time. Campus police will have direct access to the city or town's emergency services and can coordinate or assist if authorities are required on campus.

IPSE RESOURCES

As discussed in chapters 3 and 4, an inclusive postsecondary education (IPSE) program is a special college program for individuals with intellectual and developmental disabilities who do not have a traditional high school diploma and for whom the traditional college degree route is not possible. The goals of IPSEs are to provide independent living and employment skills. If you need financial assistance, it is important to pay attention to whether or not the IPSE is an approved comprehensive transition and postsecondary (CTP) program that is approved by the Department of Education. Only approved programs receive federal funding. IPSEs vary, but below are some resources commonly offered. Be sure to check to see which resources are available as you explore different programs.

1. **Peer mentors**: Peer mentors are often other college students paid to work as tutors throughout the semester. Students meet weekly, and peer mentors can assist with academic content, completing work, organization, or navigating campus.
2. **Residential mentors**: Universities that have residential services may provide residential mentors who provide assistance in the halls. They may assist with independent living skills like grocery shopping, laundry, making meals, or going to social events in the community or on campus.
3. **Assistive technology**: Many IPSEs are provided grant monies that allow them to purchase state-of-the-art technology that may provide you additional support and opportunities.
4. **Special classes**: Many IPSEs provide special classes that may include things like diet and nutrition, healthy relationships, functional skills like budgeting, job training, résumé building and interview practice.
5. **Vocational rehabilitation**: Since the goal of IPSE is employability, many programs are connected to the services from the office of vocational rehabilitation. The vocational rehabilitation office can provide skill and interest surveys, assist in job searches, and provide job coaching.

INFORMATION TECHNOLOGY

Each college has an office for technology support, though it may be called something other than "information technology." This office can assist you with email and online courses. It can also provide you with assistive technology and computers that may be checked out for use. Colleges typically provide a range of IT support services to students, faculty, and staff to ensure smooth operation of technology on campus. Here are some common types of IT support services offered by colleges:

1. **Help desk support**: A central help desk or IT support team is usually available to assist with general technology inquiries,

troubleshooting issues with computers, software, printers, and other devices, as well as providing guidance on accessing campus systems and resources.

2. **Network services**: Colleges manage campus-wide networks to provide internet access, Wi-Fi connectivity, and secure connections for students, faculty, and staff. IT support teams oversee network maintenance, troubleshoot connectivity issues, and implement security measures to protect sensitive data.

3. **Email and communication services**: Colleges typically offer email accounts and communication platforms for students, faculty, and staff. IT support assists with account setup, configuration, and troubleshooting email or messaging–related issues.

4. **Software support**: Colleges often provide access to a variety of software applications for academic and administrative purposes. IT support helps users with software installation, updates, licensing, and troubleshooting.

5. **Hardware support**: IT support teams may assist with hardware-related issues, including repairs, upgrades, and maintenance of computers, laptops, tablets, printers, and other devices available on campus.

6. **Classroom technology support**: Colleges equip classrooms with audiovisual technology, projectors, interactive whiteboards, and other instructional tools. IT support assists faculty and students with using classroom technology effectively and resolving any technical issues during lectures or presentations.

7. **Online learning platforms**: Colleges offer online learning platforms and learning management systems (LMS) to support online and blended (partially in person and partially online) learning environments. IT support assists with accessing, navigating, and troubleshooting issues with these platforms.

8. **Data security and privacy**: IT support teams implement security measures to safeguard sensitive data and protect against cyber threats. This includes managing firewalls, antivirus software, and data encryption, and providing guidance on best practices for data security and privacy.

9. **Training and workshops**: Colleges may offer training sessions, workshops, or online resources to educate students, faculty, and staff on IT policies, cybersecurity awareness, and best practices for using campus technology effectively and responsibly.

10. **Accessibility services**: IT support teams may provide assistance and accommodations for students, faculty, and staff with disabilities to ensure access to digital resources and assistive technologies.

These are just some of the common IT support services offered by colleges. IT helps to meet the technology needs of their campus community and facilitate teaching, learning, research, and administrative functions effectively. To find out what is offered at your institution, look on the website or contact the IT office.

CAREER SERVICES

Career services is a university or college office that provides support for all students in finding jobs. College career centers offer a variety of services to support students and alumni in their career development and job search efforts. They can provide aptitude and interest surveys to help you determine jobs that you might be good at; provide resources for job fairs; provide job application assistance; schedule mock interview practice sessions; and help make job connections. Here are some common services provided by college career centers:

1. **Career counseling and advising**: Career counselors provide one-on-one guidance to students and alumni, assisting them in exploring career options, identifying their strengths and interests, and developing career goals and plans.
2. **Résumé and cover letter assistance**: Career centers assist with résumé and cover letter writing, including providing feedback on content, formatting, and customization for specific job opportunities.
3. **Job search strategies**: Career advisors help students and alumni develop effective job search strategies, including networking techniques, online job search methods, and utilizing job boards and career resources.
4. **Interview preparation**: Career centers conduct mock interviews and provide coaching to help students and alumni prepare for job interviews. This may include practicing common interview questions, discussing interview techniques, and receiving feedback on performance.

5. **Career workshops and events**: Career centers organize workshops, seminars, and events on various career-related topics such as job search strategies, résumé writing, interview skills, networking, and professional development.
6. **Career assessments**: Some career centers offer career assessment tools and resources to help students explore their interests, skills, values, and personality traits, and how they relate to different career paths.
7. **Internships and experiential learning opportunities**: Career centers assist students in finding internships and experiential learning opportunities relevant to their field of study or career interests. They may provide resources for researching and applying to internships, as well as guidance on maximizing the learning experience.
8. **Career fairs and networking events**: Career centers organize career fairs, networking events, and employer information sessions where students and alumni can connect with employers, learn about job opportunities, and expand their professional networks.
9. **Graduate school preparation**: For students considering further education, career centers offer resources and guidance on researching graduate programs, preparing application materials, and navigating the graduate school admissions process.
10. **Alumni career services**: Many career centers extend their services to alumni, providing career counseling, job search assistance, and professional development support to help alumni advance in their careers or make career transitions.

These services are designed to empower students and alumni to make informed decisions about their career paths, develop job search skills, use their education, and successfully transition into the workforce or pursue further education.

COUNSELING SERVICES

Counseling services on college campuses often aim to provide comprehensive mental health support to students. Here are some common counseling services that are typically available:

1. **Individual counseling**: Students can schedule one-on-one sessions with a licensed counselor or therapist to address personal, academic, or mental health concerns. These sessions are private and confidential.

2. **Group counseling**: Some counseling centers offer group therapy sessions where students with similar concerns can come together in a supportive environment to discuss and explore shared experiences.

3. **Crisis intervention**: Counseling centers often provide crisis intervention services for students experiencing urgent mental health crises or emergencies. This may include immediate support, risk assessment, and referrals for further care, if needed.

4. **Psychiatric services**: Some counseling centers have psychiatrists or psychiatric nurse practitioners who can provide psychiatric evaluations, medication management, and ongoing mental health support.

5. **Workshops and seminars**: Counseling centers may organize workshops, seminars, or programs on various topics such as stress management, mindfulness, coping skills, and relationship dynamics.

6. **Outreach and prevention programs**: Counseling centers may engage in outreach activities to raise awareness about mental health issues and promote emotional well-being across the campus community. This might include table events, awareness campaigns, and collaboration with student organizations.

7. **Online and teletherapy services**: Many counseling centers offer online counseling or teletherapy options, allowing students to access support remotely through phone or video sessions.

8. **Referrals**: In cases where students require specialized or long-term care beyond what the counseling center can provide, counselors can offer referrals to off-campus mental health professionals or community resources.

College is full of new experiences and sometimes they can feel overwhelming! It's good to familiarize yourself with the counseling services available on campus. If you feel like you need some help, reach out. That's what they are there for! Many colleges prioritize mental health and well-being and strive to create supportive environments where students can thrive academically, emotionally, and socially.

CAMPUS MINISTRIES

Campus ministries are religious organizations or even a department typically found on college or university campuses. They offer spiritual support, community, and religious activities to students and faculty. You might seek out campus ministries that actively promote inclusion and understanding of diverse needs and find groups that prioritize creating an environment where everyone feels welcome and valued, regardless of their differences. Participation in campus ministries can offer not only spiritual guidance and support but also a sense of belonging and community. This sense of belonging and community can be especially valuable for those with disabilities as they learn, together, to navigate the college experience. By ensuring accessibility and fostering inclusivity, campus ministries can provide meaningful opportunities for spiritual growth and connection for everyone, including those with and without disabilities. Campus ministries offer a variety of services and activities to support the spiritual, social, and personal development of students, faculty, and sometimes even alumni. Here are some common services provided by campus ministries:

1. **Worship services**: Campus ministries typically organize regular worship services, including religious ceremonies, prayers, and rituals, tailored to the beliefs and practices of the affiliated faith community. These services often provide opportunities for spiritual reflection, communal worship, and fellowship.
2. **Bible studies and religious education**: Many campus ministries offer Bible studies, scripture readings, and religious education classes to deepen students' understanding of their faith traditions, explore religious texts, and engage in theological discussions.
3. **Prayer groups and meditation sessions**: Campus ministries may host prayer groups, meditation sessions, or spiritual retreats where participants can come together for prayer, reflection, and quiet contemplation in a supportive community environment.
4. **Community service and outreach**: Campus ministries often engage in community service projects, volunteer activities, and social justice initiatives to address local and global issues, promote compassion and empathy, and demonstrate the values of their faith tradition.
5. **Fellowship and social events**: Campus ministries organize social events, gatherings, potlucks, game nights, and recreational activities to foster friendships, build community, and provide opportunities

for students to connect with others who share their beliefs and values.

6. **Counseling and spiritual support**: Campus ministers, chaplains, or religious leaders affiliated with campus ministries offer pastoral care, counseling, and spiritual guidance to students facing personal challenges, seeking emotional support, or grappling with questions of faith and meaning.

7. **Retreats and spiritual retreats**: Campus ministries often host spiritual retreats or religious conferences where participants can take a break from the demands of academic life, engage in spiritual reflection, and deepen their relationship with their faith tradition.

8. **Leadership development and training**: Many campus ministries provide leadership development programs, mentorship opportunities, and training workshops to empower students to become effective leaders within their faith communities and in society at large.

9. **Interfaith dialogue and cooperation**: Some campus ministries promote interfaith dialogue, cooperation, and understanding by facilitating discussions, workshops, and collaborative projects that bring together students from diverse religious backgrounds to explore common values and shared goals.

10. **Support for international students**: Campus ministries may offer support services, cultural exchange programs, and activities specifically tailored to the needs of international students, helping them adjust to campus life, navigate cultural differences, and find a sense of belonging within the campus community.

These services contribute to the holistic development of students by providing opportunities for spiritual exploration, personal growth, community engagement, and meaningful connections with others who share their faith or spiritual beliefs.

Just as your home community provides the services its members need to thrive, the campus community provides a myriad of services designed to meet the unique needs of college students and to provide support as they face new challenges and opportunities for growth.

6

WHAT SHOULD I EXPECT?

(And What Should I *Not* Expect?)

The college environment differs in many ways from the K–12 environment. Legislation governing colleges differs from laws governing K–12 schools; therefore, you should expect your roles and responsibilities, as well as those of your family, to shift. What is needed to succeed on a college campus, specifically for out-of-class success, is directly tied to your behavior, more specifically your ability and willingness to follow policies; to be independent; to engage with campus activities; and to invest in the development of friendships. Though the level of support offered varies with the type of program, neither you nor your family should expect around-the-clock supervision. In the college environment, no one is assigned to make sure you attend class, keep up with coursework, and make healthy choices. This chapter will help you set reasonable expectations about the role of the college and your responsibilities as a college student.

In this chapter, you will learn about:

- differences between K–12 and college in terms of independence and freedom;
- areas of development: intellectual, spiritual, and identity;
- management of emotions, mature relationships, decision-making, and risk;
- safety: self, emergencies, seeking support; and
- situations: facts, challenges, tips.

WHAT IS THE SAME ABOUT COLLEGE
AND HIGH SCHOOL?

You have probably been hearing for a long time that college is very different from high school. Yet, in some ways, things are the same. You are still you. You will go to class to learn. You will have teachers (though you may call them instructors or professors). There will be rules to follow. You will be around peers who may or may not become your friends. Throughout high school, you were continually maturing and learning, and this will continue in college. However, because of the unique environment and where you are in your growth and maturing path, college can be a time when the learning and growth happen a lot faster than they did before.

WHAT IS DIFFERENT BETWEEN COLLEGE
AND HIGH SCHOOL? INDEPENDENCE!

College is different from high school in that the adults in your life now see you as a young adult. You are no longer a child! Therefore, most of the differences between college and high school are due to your new status as a young adult. Expectations are higher for adults (including you) than they are for children. In general, you will be expected to do more things independently. You will be expected to behave in ways that are socially acceptable and not detrimental to you or others. You will be expected to take care of yourself in many ways. Your first semester and even first year of college revolves around learning to manage these new expectations and becoming more and more independent. Even though you are expected to be independent, there are still plenty of resources and people available to support you, as we have discussed in previous chapters.

INDEPENDENCE

Becoming more independent revolves mostly around you being able to take care of yourself. First, you will be in charge of making sure you use basic hygiene, get yourself up for the day, go to class, and do your schoolwork. You will now decide when, how often, and what you eat; when, how often, and where you sleep; and when, how often, and where you study. Your college will not offer checks to be sure you are in your room and in bed at a certain time. Your college will not offer wake-up calls, hygiene checks, eating checks (but they do cook for you!), or homework checks. Your college will not offer an escort for travel between different campus locations or a one-on-one helper in any part of campus life. Your college will not help you keep track of your own keys or access cards to your residence hall or your room. (In fact, if you leave without your keys, they will probably charge you for having to let you into your locked room. The college will certainly charge you to replace any lost keys.) As a college student, you are expected to take responsibility for basic self-care.

Freedom management. Beyond the basics of becoming independent, managing your own freedom is also a big part of the college experience. Your college experience shapes and is shaped by how you grow and mature. You will have the freedom to decide what behavior (of yours) you consider acceptable. You will also decide who to become friends with and what is acceptable behavior from your friends. You will now decide when, how often, and where you socialize and hang out. You will decide how and where you spend your time.

While you are managing your own freedom, there will be rules within which you are expected to operate. Every college has a set of rules, also called a code of conduct or an honor code, that you will be expected to follow. Many of the rules will be what you might expect. Some of the rules will reflect your state's laws. In some ways, the rules will also reflect the type of institution you attend. All of the rules will be listed within the student handbook. All of the rules in the student handbook, if broken, will be addressed by campus staff and dealt with through a specific process. Some rules, if broken, will be referred to the local police, such as illegal drug use and most crimes. Many public colleges have to refer alcohol policy violations to the local police, while private institutions typically address liquor violations in-house. We will address the college conduct process later in this chapter. Even though there will be plenty of rules, and, of course, laws to follow, you still have the freedom to decide to follow them or manage the consequences of not following them.

AREAS OF STUDENT DEVELOPMENT

There is a whole field of study dedicated to understanding more about college students and their growth during the college years. Most college students go through predictable changes as part of their college experience. Our understanding of these changes is described by something called student development theory. These are models that explain how college students grow and mature. We can use these models to understand and support all of the ways that college students manage their freedom and independence.

Intellectual development: Intellectual development in college students describes brain structures that allow for the specific and ordered stages of growth that one goes through. Once a stage is completed, the brain is different, so there is no going back to a previous stage. Stages build upon each other and get more complex as students mature. For instance, consider an early stage for babies. If a toy is covered with a blanket, the baby will think it no longer exists. Then, once the baby grows intellectually, he or she will reach a new stage where he or she knows to look for it under the blanket. Once the baby realizes that the object doesn't stop existing just because it is hidden, there is no going back to the first stage. Once you know something, you know it. In your college experience, this area covers your ability to understand and use abstract concepts from your courses; developing some specific skills and then getting good at them; and making sound decisions that involve a certain level of risk. Examples are learning to manage your time well and learning to follow the rules.

Spirituality development: Spirituality development describes the stages you may go through to answer big questions about the meaning of life. *Why am I here? What is my purpose in life?* College students begin to develop through stages that may take a lifetime to experience. Most students start with accepting the truth as it is presented to them by adults. Students will then test, question, and explore different ideas. They may begin to settle on and commit to a specific way to make meaning of the world that they align with for specific and clear reasons.

Social identity development: Social identity development addresses your race, ethnicity, gender, sexual orientation, and even your abilities. These are all part of your identity, or how you describe yourself. Some categories are more pronounced than others at different times in your growth. Identity development is the process you will go through to come to see yourself as a person who is part of any and all of these categories. Most college students go through stages of defining their identity, separate from their family. When part of your identity is in the minority on campus, oftentimes there is a club that can help you make connections to others who share that specific part of your identity. There are clubs that focus on culture or race and ethnicity, clubs that focus on people of a specific sexual orientation, clubs that focus on gender, and some campuses may have clubs that focus on disability, such as students with autism. Clubs that bring students who have a common identity together can be a great benefit because they provide support, education, and potential friendships, which can lead to an increased sense of belonging.

You will be developing in many areas at the same time. It is very exciting! But sometimes, it can be a little overwhelming. Many times, the development process includes a phase of discomfort. You can think of it like this: First, you are moving right along, and everything is fine. Then you get some sort of input or information dropped into your world that challenges or does not match what you already think or feel. Once that happens, you eventually move into a phase where you may reexamine your current thinking. You think about it. You ask questions. You may test things out. Then, once you settle on what to think or feel, you will begin to transform into a new stage or way of thinking. It is at that time that you will begin to feel a leveling off to a smooth state again.

While all of this development is happening, you are living with and interacting with other people who are also going through their own development. The action of managing your emotions and managing relationships with others can be a perfect source of the input needed to move from one stage of development to another. As you move through your day, you can't help but experience emotions and encounters with other people. You will never think, "Ah, that irritation is a necessary input for me to develop and progress to the next stage of growth." But that will be what is happening.

MANAGING EMOTIONS

Managing emotions is a big part of everyday life. College is about growth. Being exposed to different viewpoints assists with that growth. Most of your college peers are learning these things at the same time you are, which can lead to challenges. Being able to manage your own emotions when confronted with opposing opinions is necessary. If emotions are not managed appropriately, it can not only have negative consequences for you in the area of conduct but also in the area of friendship.

Take the time before you start college to reflect on how you manage your emotions now and in what areas you wish to grow. What you do with your emotions in college is key to your success, as emotions often trigger behaviors. Are you aware of how you are feeling, or do you try to ignore your feelings? Do you hold on to them, or have you learned techniques to help you process them and move on? How do you react when you are angry? When you are disappointed? Frustrated? Really excited? Tired? Hangry? An important campus resource to assist with learning to manage emotions is the college counseling center (which is different from the counseling academic department for students learning to be counselors). The college counseling center typically offers individual counseling sessions as well as group sessions. Many times, this department offers educational programs such as assertiveness training or anger or grief management.

MANAGING MATURE RELATIONSHIPS

Managing your emotions will tie directly into the relationships you are able to develop. In college, you will develop relationships with roommates or hallmates, classmates, friends, staff, and faculty (your professors/instructors). You will also continue to develop your relationship with your family, even when you are in college. You will always be somebody's child, but you will now begin your journey of being an adult in those relationships. Sometimes families have a hard time seeing college students as adults, especially within the same timeframe students see themselves. How you manage your newfound freedoms will impact how quickly and smoothly your family changes how they view you.

MANAGING FRIENDSHIPS

Developing friendships involves many things. Your ability to have appropriate interactions is very important to any other person you are with. Everyone wants to be able to trust the people they are friends with; they want to trust that they are safe, that they can be at ease, and that they aren't at risk of being made fun of or embarrassed. The ability to have a conversation that is balanced or equal between you and the person you are speaking with is important. This ability requires your awareness of how much you are sharing about yourself and making sure you allow the other person to share, as well. Having the capacity to understand your own emotions, as well as being able to understand someone else's emotions, is also important. People seek to feel understood and cared about, and being able to contribute those things to a friendship is important. Another major factor in successfully managing friendships is understanding boundaries—both yours and others. Know what boundaries you won't allow others to cross. Also, be able to recognize, respect, and comply with other peoples' boundaries. Next, the ability to talk about those boundaries before anyone crosses them is a key self-awareness practice that will allow a healthy relationship to develop. If you have trouble with social communication, spending time learning about this area before going to college will be helpful.

MANAGING DECISION-MAKING ABILITIES AND RISK

It is necessary for you, as a college student, to have the ability to make good decisions about taking appropriate risks. It is also important to understand the norms of your college. First, remember that everyone makes mistakes throughout their lives, and no one is expecting any college student to never make a poor decision. In fact, a lot of learning can happen due to poor decisions. However, you do need to be able to make the majority of your decisions result in maintaining your safety, even when they involve decisions about how to have fun. This section brings together all the other sections we talked about above, such as healthy relationships, independence, and managing freedom, and it also ties into later sections, such as peer pressure.

You may easily come into contact with friends who are thinking of creative, and possibly dangerous, ways to have fun. It is not uncommon for college students to literally decide to jump off the local bridge and swim in the river, for example. You may also be in a situation where you need to make decisions about pranks or practical jokes. Sometimes pranks are fun and harmless, but most times, they escalate into activities that cause property or physical damage. In addition, they can diminish the level of trust in friendships. It is also very possible that you will be in a situation where you need to decide whether or not to use any number of substances, such as alcohol or drugs.

Another category of decision-making is regarding your classes and studies. You can decide to go to every class session, or you can decide to skip one or more of them (which is not recommended). Most professors assign points for class attendance and participation that count toward students' final grade; so in this way, students are held accountable for skipping class. However, no one will remind you or force you to attend. Just keep in mind that if you decide to skip class, you will likely miss a great deal of information that you will still be responsible for knowing.

Tip: If you miss a class, don't ask the professor what you missed and then expect him or her to fill you in or provide notes. It is your responsibility to find out!

MANAGING PEER PRESSURE

When getting to know peers and developing friendships, you may face peer pressure in certain situations. Peer pressure is when others, usually around your age, will verbally and emotionally try to get you to do something you may not have thought of on your own, that you may not be interested in doing, or that you simply do not want to do. You need to be able to make decisions that are best for your well-being. Some peer pressure is harmless, and some may even be positive. For instance, you may face peer pressure from friends coaxing you to take a study break in order to go out to dinner together. But some peer pressure can be dangerous and have nothing to do with friendship. For instance, you may face peer pressure to do something illegal in order to prove to a potential friend that you are worth his or her time. (Remember—no one needs to prove anything in order to be someone's friend.) You need to be able to gauge the situation and stand up for yourself with a level of assertiveness that matches the situation. For example, saying "no" to an invitation to dinner calls for a very different level of assertiveness than saying "no" to something illegal intended to prove your worth.

MANAGING SAFETY

Safety can be divided into several categories. Keeping yourself safe is one category. Emergencies, or crises, is another. Getting caught breaking a rule, perhaps doing something unsafe for you or others, is a third category of safety called "student conduct."

Self-safety: Friendships, decision-making ability, and peer pressure all tie into the topic of trusting others and your safety. Your ability to avoid being a victim of someone else's harmful intent is very important to your college experience and to the rest of your life. Do you think you might have any behaviors that could possibly lead to being taken advantage of or being targeted by a bully? Many college students seem to think of themselves as invincible, but no one is. Colleges offer a range of programs that promote safety prevention to help students be more aware of their surroundings, of other people, and of dangers. Programs can include topics such as online safety, self-defense, and learning about assault prevention in consensual sexual relationships. Students with self-harm behaviors such as cutting or disordered eating are encouraged to work with the counseling center. Sometimes those behaviors are not only unhealthy for the students themselves but can also be very disruptive to the student's group of friends.

WHAT TO DO IN AN EMERGENCY

Your school will have staff trained to manage crises and emergencies. Some crises involve only one or two people, such as an assault or a suicide attempt. Some crises involve the entire campus, such as a shooter. In all cases, calling your college's campus police office is a good choice. You can also call 911. Anytime you would call 911, you should also contact campus authorities. However, if something has happened and it doesn't feel like an emergency worthy of the police or an ambulance, then you can go to school staff for help (for example, the resident assistant (RA) or the dean of students. Do you think you can tell the difference between the level of urgency or danger involved in contacting the appropriate people? Here's a chart to help you:

Table 6.1   Emergency type and appropriate contact

Example of an Emergency	Call 911	Call Campus Police	Seek Staff Help
A pipe breaks in your building, and water is gushing everywhere.		x	x
You are locked out of your room, and you really have to use the bathroom or need an assignment in the room that is due in minutes.		x	x
You see a fire starting to smolder.	x—and pull the alarm		
You see a fender bender (very minor car accident) on campus.		maybe	
You see an accident on campus, and it seems like someone might be hurt.	x		
Your roommate was out drinking earlier, and now you can't wake them up.	x		
You think you smell pot in your hallway.		x	x
You are having a panic attack.			x

SEEKING SUPPORT OR HELP (NONEMERGENCY)

In high school, if you were in need of help with nonemergencies like improving your study skills or managing emotions, you may have been contacted by the school employees to get connected to sources of support. In college, however, no one will initiate contact. If you want help or support, you must take the first step and ask for it. It is your choice to seek help and to disclose any disability to the college staff. Once you decide to request help, and then actually ask for it, you'll be instructed to follow the college's paperwork requirements. After a review to see what is appropriate, the college must provide you with the support discussed in previous chapters regarding the disability. The college also has many other supports that you have the choice to use or not. No one will force or require you to use the supports. You may request help in improving your study skills or in understanding an instructor's instructions. You may ask for help with the emotions you are dealing with. You may ask for help with getting involved on campus so you can make some new friends.

As stated in chapter 3, remember that the type of college you attend will make a difference in your experiences. Colleges offer different levels of support depending on their resources and their focus on individual care. Most colleges offer tutoring and writing services, health services, counseling, reasonable academic accommodations for courses, acceptance of service and support animals, fun events and educational events to participate in or to help run, and clubs to join and participate in, and some colleges have peer mentoring programs.

Tip: Take advantage of campus activities and clubs! These events offer many opportunities to make friends!

Tip: Develop a relationship with the staff in the office of disability services. While they are not required to do everything you ask, they are in their roles because they care about students and want them to succeed. As they get to know you, they may have tips and guidance on sources of support that may be helpful and contribute to your positive experience.

Consider the support that can and cannot be provided. The federal law, called FERPA, states that as a college student, you are considered an adult with control over your own records. Depending on the situation, the college staff can only share student record information with families (or anyone the student designates) if the student gives specific permission, which involves signing a form. As discussed in chapter 2, the college will not provide you with a personal assistant or change the content of a course.

Your college must provide web content accessibility, allow animals on campus (with emotional support and service animals), and have a process to provide reasonable accommodations discussed earlier, inside and outside of the classroom.

Being aware of your strengths and areas for growth will help you transition and thrive in college. Understanding that you will develop in specific areas of your life and that there will be ups and downs as you progress through your experience will help you cope on your journey. Now, we will consider some of the specific situations you will face in college.

LIVING ON CAMPUS

The Facts

- Generally, students share living arrangements.
- In any residence hall and even individual rooms, there is typically a lot of sensory input to manage.
- University staff enter students' rooms a few times throughout the academic year. Sometimes they will tell you ahead of time, but other times they will show up unannounced and enter whether or not you are there. Residence hall staff are required to do routine checks of the condition of the room. Also, maintenance will enter the room in order to fix any problems.
- University furniture is assigned to each room and typically has rules about not moving it out.
- In most cases, you will be expected to share a bathroom. Sometimes you will share with one other person, sometimes with three to 10 other people, and sometimes with the entire floor of 50 people.
- Many residence halls are not separated by gender, by building, by floor or even by room. Depending on your college, the level of privacy may be different from what you assume and from what you have at home.
- Learning to get along with others in a new environment is part of the growth process. It can also lead to fulfilling friendships.

POTENTIAL CHALLENGES

- Intense or monopolizing behaviors or not understanding humor can result in roommate troubles. Unaddressed, these behaviors can lead to one roommate avoiding the other or moving out. Some students share access to their location with friends via their phone. Constantly checking someone's location or accusing your roommate of turning their locator off without telling you are behaviors that will lead to conflict.
- Maybe you are someone who holds stress in all day and then releases stress after you get back to your own space. Behaviors to release stress may include flapping, vocalizing, pacing, and so on. Some behaviors, especially if not discussed ahead of time, may cause alarm if not understood. Working with the staff (housing and perhaps campus safety) and your roommate proactively can help set expectations and provide reassurance ahead of time. This will set you up for a more harmonious roommate relationship.
- One key to a successful relationship is understanding boundaries and the appropriate balance of respecting someone else's privacy and interacting with them. Privacy can mean not watching your roommates changing their clothes, not listening to phone conversations, not eating their food, and not using their things.
- There are a lot of benefits to living in a room without a roommate (a single room), but it is not always for the best. In many cases, having a single room leads to loneliness and isolation since it limits the interactions you have with others and, as a result, the potential for close and lasting friendships.

TIPS AND SUPPORT

- If you live on campus, the college provides a resident assistant (RA) on every floor. An RA is a student staff member who lives in the general living area. The RA will help with community-building and roommate conflicts, fix anything wrong with the room, assist in emergencies, and enforce policies.
- One way to manage your sensory level on move-in day is to request an early move-in to lessen the activity around you.
- If you wish to live on campus but know that you will be successful only if certain things are in place, you can seek information from

the residence life office while you are making your college decisions. Specific room accommodations can often be granted, depending on the situation. Most colleges have a specific process for seeking such accommodations, but these can vary. Some options will have an additional cost. Typical requests include issues with sound level, animal exposure, mobility, and access to a private bathroom.

- Regarding animals: proactively advocate for yourself and do not depend on the college staff to communicate between offices. They may, but they may not. Instead, you should inform the office of disability services, and you should also provide copies of the paperwork to the housing and residence life office regarding any special room arrangements or animal permissions. Once you have permission for the support animal, we encourage you to tell your soon-to-be roommate, so it is not a surprise. Some people have a fear of certain animals. You don't want to be matched with someone who will be upset by your support animal and move out within a few days. Though difficult situations can be worked through, losing one roommate and getting to know a new one can be disruptive and disappointing, especially while you are transitioning to the newness of college. Unlike service animals, a wide variety of animals can serve as support animals. Depending on what your service animal actually is, the chance of a roommate not wanting to live with it may be higher if the animal is a tarantula or a snake versus a dog or cat. On the other hand, you may be matched with a student who also has an approved service or support animal.

ACCOUNTABILITY AND THE STUDENT CONDUCT PROCESS

The Facts

- The student conduct system is based on educating students by holding them accountable for behaviors that violate policy, regardless of the reasons for the behaviors.
- As stated earlier, college policies (rules) are listed in the student handbook. They cover laws and rules that set the groundwork for a healthy campus community where students can thrive.

- Many colleges have a rule banning disruptive behaviors. Examples of disruptive behaviors include:
  - being chronically late to class;
  - interrupting or leaving before the end of class;
  - having inappropriate conversations with peers (i.e., avoid resulting in being perceived as too aggressive, threatening, or stalkerish); and
  - not taking care of oneself (basics of hygiene, eating, sleeping, and substance use).
- Each college has a well-defined process that students go through to examine what happened, who is responsible, and how to reach a resolution. The process can be found in detail in the student handbook. The student handbook describes each step that the college will take and your rights as a student.
- Often, a minor policy violation will result in a one-on-one conversation with a staff member. If found responsible, a student may have to complete an assignment designed to help him or her learn something about the topic.
- Consequences from a conduct process cannot force you to disclose your disability. However, the college may encourage you to do so, with the goal of helping you get connected to resources that will better support you as you move forward.
- The protections from Section 504 disability law do not give any special allowance for students with disabilities to use illegal drugs or alcohol. Students with disabilities will be held accountable for breaking the rules just as any other student would be. Of course, in some states, marijuana is legal. However, even if your college is located in one of those states, it will have policies to follow that may prohibit its use on campus.
- There will be two different conduct processes: one for any sexual or gender-related policy violations (Title IX) and one for everything else. Some colleges also have a separate process for any other form of discrimination.

POTENTIAL CHALLENGES

- Being able and willing to control your behavior is key to your college experience. For example, you must be able to follow the rules and deal with the consequences of breaking them.

- Your family is not permitted to be directly involved in the conduct process.
- Being held responsible for multiple policy violations, meaning a student shows a pattern of breaking the rules, can possibly lead to loss of privileges and possible suspension.

TIPS AND SUPPORT

- If you are not able to understand something in the conduct process, you can request support. Most likely, that support will come from the staff in the office of disability services.
- The staff that manage the conduct process are in their jobs because they care about students and want to see them thrive. No one is deliberately seeking to give you a hard time or treat you unfairly.
- If you do feel that you have been treated unfairly, you may appeal a decision. The conduct process includes an appeal process.

ORGANIZATIONAL, PLANNING, AND TIME MANAGEMENT SKILLS

The Facts

- Along with your new freedom comes responsibilities. College students are expected to manage their own time and tasks.
- There is a lot to manage in several different areas of life: schoolwork, taking care of yourself, free time, and socializing.
- Failure to manage your responsibilities will have consequences that you must deal with. For example, failing to go to class will impact your grade. If attendance is part of the course grade, you can't get those points back once they are lost. Also, it is unfair to expect the professor or other students to "give you" what you missed.
- No one will tell you when to start or stop doing something, such as when you should start studying, start sleeping, stop procrastinating, and stop playing video games.
- Fifteen credits (or five classes) can take up to 15 hours a week of in-class time. However, each class will also require out-of-class time to read, study, and complete assignments. For five classes, that can mean an additional 30 hours a week or more. That means that the time

you will put into your academics will be similar to the time that goes into a full-time job.

Potential Challenges

- There will be many weeks when you have a lot to accomplish. Managing multiple priorities or tasks can require deliberate action, such as planning and sticking to your plan. You cannot depend on other people to keep track of what you need to do.
- At first, you may stumble and make mistakes with your planning and organizing, but most people expect that the transition to college takes some time. The important part is to keep trying and not give up if your first strategy does not work.

Tips and Support

- If you don't already use one, start using some sort of calendar or planner to mark all the places you need to be and the tasks you want to complete. Then develop a habit of looking at the calendar or planner every day.
- Break larger assignments into smaller tasks. Use your planner to examine due dates for assignments and then schedule work time in the days leading up to the due date. This helps to ensure you have enough time to complete something well—even if things happen that you weren't expecting, like a special event, illness, or a family emergency.

ACADEMICS

The Facts

- Your grades (also referred to as your grade point average, GPA, quality point average, QPA) matter! Some majors will not allow you to continue in that major unless you keep your grades above a certain level. To stay in college and keep your financial aid, students usually need to stay above a 2.0 GPA. If you receive a poor grade in a class, this will affect your GPA throughout your time in college, and it will appear on your transcript unless you retake the course. Keep in mind that your GPA and transcripts are often things a prospective employer will consider when making a decision about whether or not to hire you.

- Readings and assignments are crucial to passing a course. You should plan to complete every assignment that is listed in the syllabus, even if the instructor does not remind you to do it. Most instructors require reading outside of class, and they expect you to understand the material. They may not directly review the reading material in class. Instead, they may build upon what you have read and use it as a starting point for the lecture and/or in-class activities.
- Allowing tasks to pile up until the last minute will generally result in lower-quality work, which will be reflected in your grade.
- Strong students use campus resources, like the tutoring center and the writing center.

Potential Challenges

- Students can run into trouble with their academics when they fail to read instructions, fail to notice due dates (or think of them as suggestions), or assume certain parts of class have more importance (or course points) than others. For example, class participation can count as a major part of your overall course grade. Not attending class, or attending class but barely participating, may result in failing a course even if you do well on all the other assignments. Look carefully at the syllabus before you begin the course to ensure that you understand how your grade will be calculated.
- Skipping class on purpose (e.g., playing video games instead) or by accident (oversleeping) will not lead to success. You need to be responsible and have the self-discipline to tear yourself away from something you are engaged in so that you can get to class on time.
- Thinking you are good at multitasking usually doesn't lead to success in college-level coursework. Most people are not good at splitting their focus between two or more activities. Therefore, planning to study for an exam while you are at a basketball game is probably not a good idea.

Tips and Support

- Reach out and make connections. There are many benefits to forming relationships with your instructors and fellow students and fully engaging in your classes. Not only will you understand and learn the material better but you will feel a stronger connection to the course and the program. Also, you will likely find that you enjoy yourself! Talk with your instructors during their office hours. Join a study group for one or more of your classes.

- Utilize your college's supports such as the tutoring center, the writing center, and the library employees.
- Review the syllabus for each of your courses to understand all requirements. Each course will be different.
- Think about the environment in which you study and learn best. It may be in your room with other people, or it may be alone, somewhere quiet. It may be while listening to music. It may be somewhere with few distractions. Most likely, you will be more alert at a particular time of day. Be intentional about when and how you study.
- If you notice that you have some days where multiple projects are due at the same time, you need to: (1) plan ahead to get them done, and (2) talk with your instructors to explore the option of completing some of the tasks early. Having many projects due at once is not a reason to request an extension on an assignment.
- Reflect every few weeks on how you think you are doing. Ask for feedback from your instructors. Take action on the feedback they give you to improve your learning.
- If you start to realize that you are not doing well in any course, it is best to reach out for help sooner rather than later. When you ask for help earlier in the semester, then there is time to connect you with different resources. When you wait until the end of the semester, or even after a class is over, then there is no time to provide you with help. An instructor will not go back in to change your grades because you admit or recently realized that you should have used the tutoring center. Supports guaranteed to you because of a disability cannot be retroactive, meaning that if you ask for support late in the semester, the grades you already received up to that point will not be impacted.

Fun Facts

- It is not uncommon for students to study abroad. If you are interested, talk to the staff in your office of disability services and the study abroad office to learn about the expectations and whether or not it is a good fit for you and the program you are in.

- There is a national honor society for students with disabilities called Delta Alpha Pi. The honor society is for students who either self-identify as individuals with disabilities or have presented documentation of a disability to the office of disability services. To qualify, students need to complete approximately eight courses and have a 3.1 GPA or higher.

Many people look back on their college experience and remember it as fun. It is a time when you will be surrounded by a lot of people who are similar to you in a lot of ways, mainly people who are becoming independent and preparing for a career. Learning new things is fun, meeting new people and developing new friendships is fun. You will manage your own freedom, and that can lead to many enjoyable experiences. But there will also be days when college doesn't feel like fun at all. You will have days of uncertainty. You will have days when you feel like you have way too much to do, and you are not sure how you will get it all done. But, through it all, you will be growing in many important ways. As discussed in this chapter, going through the developmental stages and learning to manage emotions and relationships can be a little messy and uncomfortable. One day you may look back with many fond memories, but while you are going through the actual growth, you may experience a wide range of emotions.

7

NEW ROLES AND RESPONSIBILITIES

What Are Your New Responsibilities and What Is the Role of the Parents/ Caregivers of a Postsecondary Student?

As you transition from K–12 to postsecondary education, changes in the role of the school and your responsibilities as a student can be unsettling. Sometimes the shift in the roles and responsibilities can be downright scary—especially for the unprepared! This chapter will help you understand your new responsibilities. It will also help your family evaluate how your needs and circumstances will mesh with the institution's resources and the expectations within the campus culture. This chapter also helps families better understand how *their* role changes as you enter postsecondary education. In addition, this chapter provides strategies to help your parents support you effectively in your changing responsibilities.

Topics in this chapter include:

- the new adult responsibilities of the student;
- how roles shift from parent to student; and
- what an appropriately supportive parent/caregiver looks like.

STUDENT: NEW RESPONSIBILITIES

College is different from your previous K–12 experience. You are now an adult, so your education is now *your* responsibility. In elementary, middle, and high school, your parents/caregivers worked with the teachers to ensure you got the education you needed and deserved. They had parent–teacher conferences to make sure you were making progress and achieving your potential. Parents/caregivers and teachers reminded you to participate in class and to do your homework. While your parents will still be there to support and guide you, you are now the one who is responsible for your education. Although you are still a student, you are an adult, and with adulthood comes added responsibilities and choices. Below are a few things to think about concerning your new responsibilities.

Planning for Success

Guardianship: Most likely, you will have your own guardianship at the age of 18, which is another way of saying you are legally an adult. Some students who have cognitive disabilities do not have their own guardianship but have a parent or caretaker appointed by the court to be their guardian. This only happens if paperwork is completed through a lawyer and a court appoints someone as guardian. Otherwise, you are your own guardian at age 18, even if you live with your parents and/or they help you. Legally, being an adult means that you—not your parents—are responsible for your actions and the consequences that follow. This means that unless you have scholarships, financial aid, or loans, you are responsible for paying for your college expenses and doing so on time. If you have loans, you will be responsible for paying them back later. It also means if you break the policies of the college or the law, you are held responsible—not your parents. The school will ask you to make choices about things like your program and what classes you want to take. They will send you emails or letters about registration and billing statements. It will be up to you if you want to share this information with your parents and ask them for help, but you will be responsible for responding, and doing so in a timely manner.

FERPA: Family Educational Rights and Privacy Act: If you want your parents or caregivers to have access to your academic records and to be able to talk with your instructors in college, you must sign a FERPA waiver. This was discussed in chapter 2. Even with your signature on FERPA, you must be the one who requests information from your instructors and invites your parents to meetings or to talk with your instructors. Instructors will not meet at your parents' request, nor will they meet without you. Now that you are in college, involving your parents in meetings or discussions with your instructors should be rare. You are an adult and must take responsibility for advocating for yourself. While it isn't always comfortable and can sometimes be scary to ask for help, ask questions, or meet with instructors, it's an important part of growing up. Signing a FERPA waiver only *allows* the instructor to share information. It does not *require* them to do so.

To disclose a disability or not? As mentioned in previous chapters, it is your choice, not your parents', to disclose or tell the college about your disability. There will be no meetings with your parents like the individualized education plan (IEP) meetings in K–12. The college will not provide you with any support or accommodations unless you provide documentation that you have an evaluated disability that will impact your academic success. Once you provide documentation, the office will meet with you alone to discuss necessary and appropriate accommodations. If you have not disclosed your disability to the office of disability services or received an accommodation letter to provide to your instructors, your instructors are under no obligation to provide you with additional support or assistance. Even with an accommodation letter from the office of disability services, it is still your responsibility to discuss your accommodations with the instructors ahead of time. For example, if you need extended time on an assignment, as indicated in your accommodation letter, you must talk to the instructor far enough in advance of the due date to allow him or her to make adjustments. Even with accommodation letters, the accommodations must be reasonable. For example, your instructor may provide you with two additional days to complete an assignment but not two additional weeks. That is why you must discuss ahead of time what the expectations are and what is considered reasonable. It's a good idea to make an appointment with the instructor during their office hours within the first couple weeks of class to discuss the syllabus and any accommodations and expectations. This will help you plan for upcoming assignments. You should put the due dates into your phone or planner to help you plan in advance, so you are not taken by surprise. This will also provide your instructors with valuable information about what you need to be successful. It's a good idea to schedule regular "check-ins" with your instructors to monitor your progress and ensure you are doing well and meeting the course expectations. If you wait until the end of the semester, there is little that can be done to help you improve. Remember that you pay to attend college. If you fail the class, you must retake it, which means you must also pay more money. Sometimes, if your grades fall too low, you may also lose your financial support or scholarships, so it's important to stay on top of your grades.

Self-advocacy: In college, you must be your own advocate. You must communicate with your teachers directly and make sure you understand your classes, the instructors' expectations, and the work required. You must pay attention to due dates. Many instructors do not accept late work or provide extra time. You must attend classes, participate, and do the assigned work on time and as directed. Many instructors factor attendance and participation into your final grade. No one will be there to tell you to do these things. You won't be reminded to set your alarm and go to class. You won't be reminded when you have a quiz or test or when an assignment is due. If you are having trouble, you must take the initiative to go to your instructors or seek out assistance at the tutoring center. If you work with instructors from the beginning of the class and make an effort to meet and ask questions, most instructors will do their best to provide you with support so you can be successful. However, the responsibility is now completely yours.

Now that we've reminded you of your responsibilities as a college student, we will review the roles of parents, caretakers, and families in the next section. *If you are the student, you can skip this section.*

PARENTS AND FAMILIES: NEW ROLES

The transition to adulthood and college is difficult for any parent or caregiver, but it is particularly hard for those who have a child with a disability. You have spent your life advocating for your child's access to equal and appropriate education. You've spent countless hours meeting with teachers, doctors, and other professionals, trying to do what is best and fighting for the best quality of life for your child. You've worked to help your child learn academic, social, and life skills that allow him or her to be as independent as possible and pursue a satisfying quality of life. You've held on tight, pulled your child along, and lifted him or her up when needed. You did it! Great job! You've now gotten him or her to adulthood, and it's time to allow your son or daughter to independently begin to use all those skills you've taught.

Your natural instinct as a parent/caregiver is to keep holding on and fighting for him or her. However, this is where you need to let go and allow you child to make mistakes, fail, and succeed. This is where choices and consequences serve as the teacher. Some choices may be right, and some may be wrong, but remember that we all transitioned to adulthood. We made mistakes, and we learned from them. We survived, and we learned from our failures. The challenge of letting go is not unique to parents of individuals with disabilities, but you may feel it quite strongly. Remember there are lots of staff at college who will continue to provide your child with a supportive "safety net" as he or she transitions to adulthood. Let them do their jobs!

Guide versus decision-maker: As a parent or caregiver of a child with a disability, the transition between guiding decision-making and making decisions for your child might be a bit more challenging for you. You are used to being actively involved in all aspects of your child's life, more so than most children without a disability. Your role now needs to transition from leading to guiding. Of course, you need to be interested and active in what is happening. You will no longer be the decision-maker, though, but the advisor. The student is now the decision-maker, and you will now be the guide and encourager.

Guardianship: Your child is legally considered an adult at the age of 18 and has his or her own guardianship unless you legally filed paperwork and petitioned the court to make you the guardian. If this is the case, ensure the paperwork is filed with the college so they know of your guardianship. Legally, with or without a disability, individuals who are 18 or older are now the decision-makers. They are now held responsible by law for their choices and the consequences. The college personnel will consult directly with them and will not notify you. It will be up to your child what and how much he or she discloses about what happens at college. For example, if he or she behaves in a way that violates college policies and results in disciplinary action, your child may need to go before the disciplinary review board. He or she may or may not choose to disclose the issue or the consequences to you. Since the college views the student as the legal adult, all correspondence and actions will be addressed directly to him or her. If the student is under 21 years of age, drinks, and is caught, legal ramifications from the police will be addressed directly with the student.

FERPA: Family Educational Rights and Privacy Act: FERPA protects your student's educational rights. This means anything about his or her performance in class will be addressed with him or her directly, even if you are paying the bill. Unless the student signs a FERPA form, faculty and staff are legally prohibited from sharing any student information with you. If the student misses class, you will not be notified. If he or she doesn't complete work or fails a class, you will not be notified. If they have an overdue bill and are not allowed to register for classes, you will not be notified. Even if a FERPA form is signed, you will only be included when the student requests your participation.

To disclose a disability or not? In K–12 schools, under the Individuals with Disabilities Act (IDEA), the school had a responsibility to assess students with disabilities and provide a free and appropriate education, including accommodations and modifications for academics, as well as behavioral issues. Colleges do not have this obligation. Individuals with disabilities are no longer covered under IDEA once they graduate from high school. At postsecondary institutions, the Americans with Disabilities Act (ADA) and Section 504 guarantee accessibility and protect individuals with disabilities by providing reasonable accommodations. However, for these protections, individuals with disabilities must self-disclose to the disability services office of their college. Individuals must provide documentation of the disability and work with the office to determine reasonable accommodations, such as extended time for assignments or testing in a separate setting. These supports will not include 1:1 tutoring or assistance, nor will they be as individualized and intensive as in K–12. Colleges are only required to provide what is reasonable. There are no accommodations in college for behavioral support. So, if your child had an IEP for emotional behavior disorders and a behavioral intervention plan, these will not be implemented in college. All students must be safe to themselves and others, act appropriately in community settings, and be nondisruptive in class, among residents in the residence halls, and on campus. Your child must understand that he or she ultimately has the choice to disclose or not. If your child does not disclose, he or she will receive nothing beyond the support traditional students receive. There is no going back after the fact and asking for a "redo."

Prior to admission to college, discuss disability disclosure with your child, and explain the pros and cons. If he or she chooses to disclose, help your child to locate the appropriate office. He or she will need to meet individually with the office of disability services staff, but it is helpful if to know what supports are needed prior to the meeting. Again, by law, the college is only obligated to provide accommodations for what is reasonable within the context of the course and only if documentation is provided. The accommodations and supports cannot change the content of the course. Accommodations can only support the student in accessing the content and being successful.

Self-advocacy: Unlike in K–12, where you advocated for your child at IEP meetings and to classroom teachers, it is now time for your child to advocate for him or herself. He or she is now considered an adult and must be able to talk with the staff and faculty at the college to clarify misunderstandings and ask for assistance when needed. You can provide guidance and encouragement about who he or she should seek assistance from, but ultimately, it is their responsibility. Even with a signed FERPA form, instructors will not meet or talk with parents without the student present. Hopefully, your child knows and understands what supports help the most and can request these supports from the services and personnel provided on campus. Beyond the office of disability services, career centers offer interest surveys, job fairs, and career counseling. Tutoring centers provide specific support for coursework. Writing centers provide assistance in writing research papers or essays. Counseling centers offer individual and group mental health counseling and/or social groups. It's important to know what services the college provides and to guide your child to the appropriate service to seek assistance. (See chapter 5 for more information about the support services commonly provided by colleges and universities.)

Possible Resources

First-time college students with disabilities may need several resources and supports to ensure a successful transition and experience in college. Here are some key considerations and resources that may be needed:

1. **Disability services office**: Every college is required by law (under the Americans with Disabilities Act and Section 504 of the Rehabilitation Act) to have a disability services office. This office coordinates accommodations and support services for students with disabilities. It's essential for students to register with this office early in their college career to establish accommodations.
2. **Accommodations**: Accommodations are adjustments made to ensure that students with disabilities have equal access to education. These may include extended time on tests, note-taking services, accessible classroom materials, preferential seating, or the use of assistive technology. The specific accommodations needed will vary based on the students' disability and individual needs.
3. **Accessibility**: Colleges should provide accessible facilities, including accessible classrooms, housing options, dining halls, and recreational facilities. It's important for students to communicate any specific accessibility needs to the disability services office.
4. **Support networks**: Building a support network is crucial. This can include disability support groups, peer mentors, faculty advisors, and counselors who can provide guidance and assistance throughout the college experience.

5. **Transition planning**: Developing a transition plan that addresses academic, social, and personal goals can help students with disabilities navigate the challenges of college life. This plan may include setting academic goals, identifying potential challenges, and outlining strategies for success.

6. **Technology and assistive devices**: Depending on the disability, students may require specific technology or assistive devices to support their learning and daily activities. This could include screen readers, speech-to-text software, magnification tools, or mobility aids.

7. **Advocacy skills**: Teaching students self-advocacy skills empowers them to communicate their needs effectively to professors, advisors, and support staff. This includes knowing their rights, understanding their disability, and requesting accommodations when necessary.

8. **Emotional and mental health support**: College can be a stressful time for any student, and students with disabilities may face additional challenges. Access to counseling services, support groups, and mental health resources is important for overall well-being.

9. **Financial planning**: Understanding the financial aspects of college, including tuition, fees, and potential financial aid opportunities specifically for students with disabilities, is essential. Financial planning can help alleviate stress and ensure that students have the resources they need to succeed.

10. **Career services**: Access to career counseling, job placement assistance, and internship opportunities can help students with disabilities prepare for their future careers. It's important for colleges to offer inclusive career services that address the specific needs and abilities of all students.

Navigating college as a first-time student with disabilities requires careful planning, advocacy, and support. By accessing available resources, building a support network, and developing necessary skills, students can successfully transition to college and thrive academically, socially, and personally.

Tips for Parents and Caregivers in Transitioning
a Student with Disabilities to College

Transitioning to college can be both exciting and challenging for any student, and for parents of children with disabilities, there are some specific considerations that can help make the process smoother:

1. **Know your child's rights**: Familiarize yourself and your child with the services provided under the Americans with Disabilities Act (ADA) and Section 504 of the Rehabilitation Act. Colleges are required to provide reasonable accommodations to students with disabilities. Chapter 2 provides more information on the laws governing higher education.
2. **Start early**: Begin researching colleges and their disability support services well in advance. Some colleges have better resources and support systems for students with disabilities than others.
3. **Involve your child**: Encourage your child to take an active role in the transition process. This includes visiting campuses, talking to disability service providers, and advocating for his or her own needs.
4. **Build a support network**: Connect with other parents of children with disabilities who have gone through the college transition process. They can provide valuable insights and support.
5. **Understand accommodations**: Work with the college's disability services office to determine what accommodations are available and appropriate for your child. These could include extended testing time, note-taking assistance, and accessible housing.
6. **Encourage independence**: College is a time for young adults to develop independence and self-advocacy skills. Encourage your child to communicate his or her needs to professors and disability service providers directly.
7. **Prepare for emotional challenges**: Understand that transitioning to college can be emotionally challenging for any student, and even more so for students with disabilities. Be prepared to provide emotional support and encourage your child to seek counseling or support groups if needed.
8. **Financial planning**: Investigate any additional financial aid or scholarships available for students with disabilities. Some organizations offer specific scholarships to help cover the costs of accommodations and support services.

9. **Stay informed**: Keep up to date with any changes in your child's condition or needs that might affect their college experience. Regular communication with both your child and the college's disability services office is important.

10. **Celebrate achievements**: Recognize and celebrate your child's successes, both big and small, throughout the college transition process. Starting college is a major milestone, and your support can make a world of difference.

Navigating the transition from high school to college for a student with disabilities can be challenging! You may find it helpful to seek assistance from those who have worked with your child in high school, such as high school special education teachers and school counselors. By staying informed, involved, and supportive, you can help your child make the most of his or her college experience and set them up for success as they grow academically and personally.

Important Skills for Students with Disabilities Transitioning to College

Children with disabilities, like all students, benefit from developing a range of skills that can support their success in college. It is helpful to ensure that students are prepared prior to admission to college. Here are some key skills that can be particularly important for children with disabilities to work on as they prepare for college:

1. **Self-advocacy**: Teaching children how to advocate for themselves is crucial. This includes knowing their rights, understanding their disability and its implications, and effectively communicating their needs to professors, advisors, and disability services offices.

2. **Time management**: College requires managing assignments, studying for exams, attending classes, and possibly working or participating in extracurricular activities. Developing time management skills helps students stay organized and meet deadlines.

3. **Study skills**: Effective study habits, such as note-taking, summarizing readings, and preparing for exams, are essential for academic success in college. Students should also learn to adapt these skills to their specific learning styles and any accommodations they may need.

4. **Organization**: Keeping track of assignments, deadlines, and resources is crucial. This includes using planners, digital tools, or other organizational strategies that work best for the student.

5. **Adaptability**: College environments can vary widely. Teaching children how to adapt to new situations, navigate campus buildings, and adjust to different teaching styles can help them feel more confident and capable.

6. **Social skills**: Building relationships with peers, professors, and support staff is important for a fulfilling college experience. Social skills include effective communication, conflict resolution, and understanding social cues.

7. **Problem-solving**: Encouraging children to think critically and independently, solve problems, and seek help when needed fosters resilience and confidence in navigating challenges that may arise in college.

8. **Technology skills**: Many college courses and resources are accessed online. Proficiency with computers, Internet research, and assistive technology (if applicable) can enhance learning and accessibility.

9. **Emotional regulation**: College can be stressful. Teaching children strategies for managing stress, coping with setbacks, and maintaining mental well-being promotes resilience and academic persistence.

10. **Financial literacy**: Understanding basic financial concepts, such as budgeting, managing expenses, and accessing financial aid, prepares students to navigate the financial responsibilities of college life.

Talking to your child about these skills and why they are important prior to transitioning to college will be important. These skills can be developed and reinforced throughout childhood and adolescence, ideally starting early to ensure children are well prepared for the academic, social, and personal challenges of college. Parents, educators, and support professionals play a crucial role in fostering these skills and helping children with disabilities achieve their goals in higher education.

Special Considerations for Individuals With I/DD Enrolling in IPSEs

As mentioned in a previous chapter, inclusive postsecondary education (IPSE) programs admit students with developmental and cognitive disabilities who have a history of special education services K–12, did not receive a traditional high school diploma, and for whom a traditional college admission is not possible. All of the aforementioned information is helpful and applies in many respects, but most IPSEs *do* provide students with additional support. Be sure to check with the specific IPSE to determine which supports are provided.

SUPPORT PROVIDED BY IPSES

1. A program coordinator who will meet with students to do person-centered planning and determine goals for employment, independent living, and social inclusion.
2. Involvement of parents in the planning process if a student requests.
3. Support in registering with the office of disability services for accommodations.
4. Support in registering for classes and assisting instructors in making accommodations. Note: classes are usually audited classes where you go to class and complete the requirements but aren't graded.
5. Peer mentors to provide academic and social support.
6. Depending on the program, residential accommodations and residential peer mentors.
7. Internship experiences, résumé writing, and interview practice.
8. Functional skills training like budgeting, nutrition, and healthy relationships.
9. Assistance in campus and community involvement.

Prerequisite Skills That IPSEs Usually Require

For your child to be successful, a level of independence is needed. IPSEs do not provide 1:1 support or intensive support or guidance. The following skills are usually required of most IPSEs.

1. Ability to behave appropriately in a community, campus, and private setting that is safe to self and others.
2. Ability to independently navigate campus.
3. Ability to take needed medications independently if necessary.
4. Ability to ask for assistance (verbally or nonverbally) when needed.
5. Ability to interact appropriately with individuals of authority like EMTs, police officers, and university personnel.

6. Ability to use a cell phone to call or text.
7. Ability to use basic computer functions.
8. Ability to monitor one's schedule (set an alarm, get to places on time).
9. Basic hygiene skills.
10. Ability to do basic independent living skills, like keeping shared living space clean, cleaning bathrooms, doing laundry, and purchasing groceries.

This chapter provides some basic guidelines to assist students in understanding their new responsibilities and to assist parents/caregivers in more easily transitioning to their new roles. All individuals and colleges are different in their requirements and policies. These are meant as general guidelines to help you both make the transition.

8

FREQUENTLY ASKED QUESTIONS (AND ONES YOU NEED TO REMEMBER TO ASK)

This chapter includes a list of questions you and your family may have as you begin to navigate the world of postsecondary education. In addition, this chapter includes questions families and students with disabilities *should* ask as they begin to explore postsecondary options.

What is the first step in planning educational choices after high school?
The first step in planning where to go to school is clearly understanding your personal and career goals. Identifying a "just right" job and career path depends on knowing your strengths, challenges, and interests, and then setting clear and realistic goals.

Where can I find job-training resources and support as I begin exploring my postsecondary options?
Most likely, you have already worked with the Office of Vocational Rehabilitation (OVR) when you were in high school. OVR can provide continuing support for you as you continue your education. See chapter 1 for more details about how OVR can help you. Once you begin postsecondary education, most colleges have career centers that can also assist you.

I had an individualized education plan (IEP) in high school. Will I be able to get accommodations if I go to college?
Yes. Your college will have an office or a staff member that oversees requests for accommodations. Unlike K–12 schools, however, you will need to be proactive in seeking the accommodations. You will also need to follow the school's procedures for securing the accommodations you need.

The school is only required to provide "reasonable" accommodations. You can read more about this in chapter 2.

Do I have the same rights in the postsecondary environment as in my K–12 school?
Not necessarily. Some of the laws governing higher education are different from those governing K–12 schools. It is important to understand the differences in your rights and responsibilities. Chapter 2 can help you have a better understanding of the laws.

Can I be refused admission to a college due to my disability?
Any organization that receives federal money may not exclude someone from their education based on their disability.

Will I be allowed to have my service animal with me if I live in a residence hall?
The Fair Housing Act separates support and service animals. This allows residents to have an animal in a rented living space even though the owner bans animals. Therefore, support and service animals are permitted in dorms. However, you must work with the school and go through the procedures they have in place.

Do I have to disclose my disability to a college?
No. Whether or not to disclose your disability is a choice you need to make. However, keep in mind that if you do not disclose, and you later find out you are struggling in one or more classes, you cannot get accommodations retroactively. The accommodations are only for future courses.

Will my family be notified if I fail a course or get in trouble?
School personnel can only discuss your academic progress or behavior with your family if you sign a Family Educational Rights and Privacy Act (FERPA) form—even if they are paying the bill. You will need to invite your parents to any meetings between you and college personnel, but do understand that an instructor is not required to talk with your parents, even if you have a signed FERPA.

I'm thinking about taking classes online. Online courses are a lot easier than face-to-face classes, right?
That depends. If transportation and/or mobility are challenges for you, or if you need a flexible schedule due to appointments or other obligations, you may find it easier to take online classes. However, many students find online classes more difficult than face-to-face classes. Sometimes online

courses require more reading and independent work than traditional classes. Also, success in online coursework requires excellent time management skills, self-discipline, and initiative.

I'm not sure a four-year college is right for me. What other options do I have?
You have many educational options, including two-year or community colleges and vocational training programs that prepare you for a specific job. In addition, there are programs designed specifically for individuals with intellectual and developmental disabilities, including comprehensive transition and postsecondary (CTPs) programs and inclusive postsecondary education (IPSEs) programs. Learn more about choosing the program that best fits your needs in chapter 3.

I really want to continue my education so I can get a good job, but I don't have the money. How can I go to college if I can't afford it?
Because college is extremely expensive, most students receive some type of financial aid to pay for it. Financial aid is a broad term used to cover a number of different types of funding to help pay college tuition. For each college you apply to, you are awarded a financial aid package, which is a list of different types of funding you are eligible to receive. The financial aid package can be based on need, which is determined according to your family's income. It can also be based on merit, which is determined by your past performance in different areas. Each college will use your application and the completed FAFSA form to determine your financial aid package. You can learn more about financial aid and the FAFSA form in chapter 3 and at this website: https://studentaid.gov/.

How do colleges decide who gets accepted and who does not?
Colleges and universities base their admissions decisions on many factors, and different schools consider some factors more important than others. Grades are usually an important factor, but they are not the only factor. Schools sometimes look for students who have been involved in volunteer activities, sports, or clubs. Overall, schools want students who are a good fit for their campus community and who will be successful in the schools' environment.

The college program I want to take requires two math courses. I'm terrible at math! What if I have trouble passing a class?
Most colleges provide a tutoring center where students can get extra help with their classes. Don't wait until you are failing a class! Seek help early in the semester so you can get matched with a tutor.

My mom always proofread my papers when I was in high school. Now that I'm going to college, I'm worried about writing papers without having someone to look them over and make sure I don't make any silly mistakes. What can I do?
In addition to a tutoring center, most colleges provide a center to help students become better writers. This may include proofreading, but the center likely also provides workshops on topics that help students improve their writing skills.

I need absolute quiet when I study. What if I have a noisy roommate?
You and your roommate may be able to work together to figure out an arrangement that allows you to schedule some quiet time for studying. However, many residence halls are noisy places! You may need to seek out an alternative place to study. The library is usually a good option if you need a quiet space.

It's always been hard for me to make friends. I'm afraid I won't know anyone on campus, and I'll be lonely.
Be proactive! Find clubs and activities that relate to areas of interest and participate! In college, no one is likely to come and find you and encourage you to join in campus activities. You will need to take the first step, but most colleges provide many opportunities to help you meet people with similar interests.

What happens if I get sick while I am away at school?
Most schools have a health and wellness center with a nurse on staff. If you require further treatment, the nurse can help to arrange that for you.

If I take regular medication, do I need to tell the school and is there anyone to help me?
You should make health services aware of any medications you take regularly. These medications should be on file at a local pharmacy, in case you need a refill. You will need to be able to take your regular medications on your own, without assistance.

Is there anyone who can help me with my daily or weekly prescribed injections?
Depending on the health issue, sometimes you can make arrangements with the health services center to assist with more serious medications. The staff can also assist you with locating convenient needle disposal containers.

Will I have a problem using my medical marijuana on campus?
Currently, on a federal level, pot is considered in a drug category that does not allow colleges to permit its use on campus. For further information, talk with your college's dean of students, health services staff, office for disability services staff, and, if you are planning to live on campus, the residence life staff.

I've heard different things from friends and advisors about what is required to complete a college program. Who is right?
Each college has different requirements, and within each college, there are different requirements for each program. Some programs or majors will have minimum standards to meet licensing requirements set by the state. For instance, education majors may need to pass additional tests and maintain a certain grade point average (GPA). However, each individual college can require additional courses on top of the state-required minimum. Your academic advisor and the college's catalog will be able to tell you the specific requirements to complete your program.

The idea of college parties is really exciting, but I'm not sure I want to drink.
Almost every college will have groups of students who drink a lot, those who drink moderately, and also those who don't drink at all. Don't assume there is no one present who has the same interest level as you. You will be able to find people with the same interests, even if you have to look a little harder for them. Talk with your peers, with staff, and join different clubs from the start of your experience to meet a wide variety of people.

I found out I qualify for a work-study job. When will I be assigned a job?
You will not be assigned a job. You can start looking for a job by going to the college's office or web pages for the financial aid office and, possibly, the human resource office to find a list of available jobs for which to apply. Then, once you find one that looks like a good match, follow the instructions to apply for the job. A work-study job is considered part of your financial aid package because of the source of the funding to pay you. However, the people and office you will work for will expect professional and responsible behavior from their staff—including you—just like any other job. You will only get paid if you do the work that is required.

Can I start shopping now for my residence hall room?
Before you start collecting things you plan to bring to live on campus, there are a few things to check first. The residence life office will have a

list of items you are not permitted to bring. Most of the items that make that list are due to fire hazards and sometimes space considerations. Do not bring anything on the banned list, or it will be confiscated. If you will have a roommate or suitemates, you may want to be in contact with them to decide on items that your room only needs one of, or if you want to try to match decor. For instance, your college will likely limit your room to one microwave and one small refrigerator. Sometimes they require an all-in-one unit. You can plan ahead with your roommate to decide who brings what.

INDEX

ABOUT THE AUTHORS

Patricia S. Arter, EdD, is professor of special education and the department chairperson of counseling, leadership, and educational studies at Winthrop University in Rock Hill, South Carolina. She teaches graduate and undergraduate courses in special education. Dr. Arter's main areas of research are creating access for marginalized special needs populations through inclusion, vocational training, and Universal Design for Learning (UDL). Specifically, she has more than a decade of experience working with individuals with autism spectrum disorder (ASD) in the areas of vocational training, social skills training, emotional regulation training, and use of virtual reality (VR) to improve interview training skills. Before moving to Winthrop University, she founded and directed (2007–2019) the SOAR program (Students On-Campus Achieving Results), an on-campus program for individuals with ASD to secure competitive employment. Dr. Arter oversees the WinthropLIFE program (https://www.winthrop .edu/coe/winthroplife/), which offers inclusive postsecondary opportunities to individuals with intellectual disabilities through independent living, employment training, and community living. Dr. Arter has more than 20 peer-reviewed publications and numerous national and international presentations in her research areas. Prior to her career in higher education, Dr. Arter was an elementary and middle school inclusion teacher for more than 15 years.

Dr. Arter holds an EdD in special education leadership in urban-setting schools from Johns Hopkins University, an MS in special education from Johns Hopkins University, and a BS in elementary education from Towson State.

Tammy B. H. Brown, PhD, is professor of education at Marywood University. She teaches graduate and undergraduate courses in education and serves as director of the Students On-Campus Achieving Results (SOAR) program, a campus-based program to help individuals with autism spectrum disorder (ASD) to secure competitive employment. She has published numerous practitioner-focused articles in state and national journals, including a recent article in *Teaching Exceptional Children* on the use of virtual reality (VR) to prepare individuals with ASD for job interviews. She has also presented at nearly 50 peer-reviewed conferences. She is a member of the Council for Exceptional Children (CEC), the International Literacy Association (ILA), the Society for Information Technology and Teacher Education (SITE), the International Dyslexia Association, (IDA), and the Society of Children's Book Writers and Illustrators (SCBWI). She is also a member of the Keystone State Literacy Association (KSLA), where she has served on the journal's editorial board.

Dr. Brown holds a PhD in education with a concentration in literacy education from Rutgers University, an MS in reading education from Marywood University, and a BS in human ecology education from Marywood University.

Amy Paciej-Woodruff, PhD, is associate professor of education at Marywood University. She teaches in the master's and doctoral programs and has served on more than 20 dissertation committees. Research interests include male college student engagement; belonging; and online instruction. She is skilled in helping students and families in their adjustment to the college experience. She served in student affairs for 23 years in various roles at six institutions, most recently as assistant vice president for student life. There she provided leadership for housing and residence life, activities, orientation, leadership development, conduct, athletics, counseling, and student health; chaired the Behavioral Intervention Team, and served as a Title IX deputy coordinator. She is a member of the National Association for Student Personnel Administrators (NASPA), the American College Personnel Association (ACPA), and the Society for Information Technology and Teacher Education (SITE).

Dr Paciej-Woodruff holds a PhD in human development with a concentration in higher education administration from Marywood University, an MS in education in higher education administration from the University of Rochester, and a BA in psychology from Lock Haven University of Pennsylvania.

www.ingramcontent.com/pod-product-compliance
Lightning Source LLC
Chambersburg PA
CBHW021151160426
42812CB00078B/608